# CHINA'S OPENING
DOOR

# CHINA'S OPENING DOOR

## David Wall, Jiang Boke and Yin Xiangshuo

THE ROYAL INSTITUTE OF
INTERNATIONAL AFFAIRS
**International Economics Programme**

© Royal Institute of International Affairs, 1996

Published in Great Britain in 1996 by the Royal Institute of International Affairs,
Chatham House, 10 St James's Square, London SW1Y 4LE
(Charity Registration No. 208 223).

Distributed worldwide by The Brookings Institution, 1775 Massachusetts Avenue, NW,
Washington, DC 20036-2188, USA.

**British Library Cataloguing in Publication Data**
A CIP catalogue record for this book is available from the British Library.

ISBN 1 899658 14 9

Text set in Bembo.
Printed and bound in Great Britain by Redwood Books.

# CONTENTS

## Figures

## Tables

**Box**

# FOREWORD

Since the end of the 1970s, and Deng Xiaoping's rise to power, China has been engaged in a process of economic liberalization and opening up to foreign trade and investment. The process has been largely uninterrupted, even during periods of political instability and reaction such as occurred during and after the Tiananmen Square 'events'. Another period of political turbulence, surrounding the succession to Deng, has begun in 1996 and a key question for the future will be whether economic reform can remain disconnected from politics. With Chinese nationalism being given full rein it may be difficult to insulate the country's external economic policies in a cocoon of economic rationality.

China has, however, already moved a long way towards accepting the disciplines (and benefits) of international economic integration. It is already a major player in international trade and the largest recipient of direct investment outside the OECD. Negotiations to join the WTO are in train, though incomplete, and China has become active in regional fora, notably APEC.

Contributions by David Wall of the University of Sussex and by two Chinese scholars from Fudan University, Jiang Boke and Yin Xiangshuo, deal with three key elements in the 'Open Door' strategy. In his paper, David Wall writes about export processing zones. These have been used with great success for experimental liberalization – as laboratories – giving China growing confidence in its dealings with foreign investors and in international trade. They have gradually spread, in the process allowing local and provincial authorities greater policy discretion and exposure to market conditions. They have also distorted development in China, in particular pulling resources into favoured – mainly coastal – areas and creating arbitrage opportunities (and corruption) as a result of differences between export processing zones and other areas. Wall sees these zones as having reached the limit of their usefulness and argues that the creation of new zones should be resisted.

Jiang Boke describes the evolution of the system of exchange-rate management. Like the Asian 'tigers' and, earlier, Japan, China – under the economic reformers – has used devaluation as a powerful tool for stimulating exports. It has also slowly evolved from having a purely administrative system of foreign exchange allocation to one predominantly (but not totally) market-based. Jiang Boke is critical of the implementation of the reform package but supports the broad thrust of policy.

Yin Xiangshuo charts the parallel liberalization of trade policy and the way in which this has fed through into improved trade performance by Chinese enterprises, a growing role for foreign investors and a greater degree of competitiveness generally within China. The paper also underlines how far China still has to go: the assumptions behind trade policy are mercantilist, the import regime is still protectionist, and powerful vested interests in state-owned enterprises are resisting international competition.

All three papers in this volume address the fundamental question: how open is China's open door? Inevitably, there is a certain amount of overlap and, in some cases, incompatibility of data betweeen the different contributions, but together they give a valuable insight into the way policy will develop if economic reform proceeds.

*May 1996*                                                Dr Vincent Cable
                                        Chief Economist, Shell International

# ABOUT THE AUTHORS

**David Wall** is an Associate Fellow with the Asia-Pacific Programme at the Royal Institute of International Affairs and a Reader in Economics at the University of Sussex. He has been a consultant to the World Bank, OECD and the UK Overseas Development Administration on the Chinese economy. He has collaborative links with the Chinese Academy of Social Sciences in Beijing and Fudan University in Shanghai. His recent publications include *China's Long March to an Open Economy* (Paris: OECD Development Centre, 1994). He is currently associated with the work of the Chatham House China Task Force.

**Jiang Boke** is Professor of Economics at Fudan University, Shanghai, and guest Senior Research Fellow at the State Economic System Reform Research Committee, Beijing. He has degrees from Fudan University and a PhD from the University of Sussex. Since 1982, he has specialized in research into international economics and China's external financial issues. His major recent publications include *On China's Currency Convertibility*, *A Comprehensive Design of China's Money Market* and *Studies on the Impacts of RMB Exchange Rate Changes*.

**Yin Xiangshuo** is Associate Professor and Vice-Chairman of the Department of World Economy, Fudan University, where he teaches English in Economics, Development Economics, International Trade and East Asian Economy. After working on a farm for over five years during the Cultural Revolution, he entered university in 1978, graduating in English from Shanghai Teachers' College, and subsequently in economics from Fudan University, where he later took his PhD. He has published over ten papers and one book, mostly in Chinese, and has collaborated in several academic programmes, including one on China's open door policy at the University of Sussex.

# PART I

## China's Special Economic Zones

David Wall

# 1 INTRODUCTION*

Most countries have established economic zones, generally characterized by trade policies which are more liberal than elsewhere, or where
activities are permitted which are prohibited in the rest of the economy. Enterprise zones, free ports and bonded zones are found, for
example, in the United States and the United Kingdom, while most
developing countries have established export processing zones.[1]
Indeed, the fact that most of those countries which successfully followed an export-oriented strategy used such zones as part of their strategy has led many others to follow their example in establishing such
zones, or variants of the type. China is no exception.

As part of the reform programme on which China embarked in
1978, five Special Economic Zones (SEZs) were established. They have
played important and highly visible roles. In adopting this approach,
the Chinese government was aware that the most successful

---

* The research on which this paper is based was financed at different stages by the
World Bank, the OECD Development Centre, and the National Centre of
Development Studies of the Australian National University. Over the life of the
project I received a great deal of help from officials and scholars in Shenzhen,
Hainan, Xiamen and Beijing; I owe particular thanks to Dong Fureng, Li Hai Yan,
Yuan Gang Min and Wang Lina. Thanks are also due, for helpful criticism,
encouragement and support to Helen Hughes, Peter Harrold, Rajiv Lall, Kiichiro
Fukasaku and Nancy Wall. I alone am responsible for any remaining errors and for
the opinions expressed in the paper.
[1] See Wall (1976) for a discussion of the economic logic of export processing zones.
See World Bank (1993) and Warr (1989) for a review of the experience of some
countries in this respect.

economies of East and Southeast Asia had all used export processing zones in their economic liberalization programmes. Concern, among conservative leaders in Beijing, about the introduction of capitalist practices into China meant, however, that the zoning policy had the attraction of imposing geographical limits on activities involving foreigners and foreign practices. With few exceptions, such activities were limited to the SEZs until 1984.[2] Since then, with the shift in attitude to foreigners and market-based economic management practices, the number of locations in which such links are permitted has expanded as the various zones and open areas have been established. As the government of China continues to experiment with the introduction of market practices, however, some activities remain restricted to certain zones or types of zone, in particular to the SEZs (and Pudong Special Development Area, discussed below). However, as economic reform has continued and more liberal market-based policies have been applied in increasing numbers and on a wider scale, the significance of the preferential policies available in the SEZs and other zones has decreased.

The impressive performance of the SEZs, in terms of attracting investment, stimulating trade, allowing policy experimentation, and fostering overall economic growth and modernization led, quite soon after they were established, to pressure from other towns and regions wishing to establish similar zones. Apart from Hainan, the fifth zone, established in 1988, almost a decade after the original four, the government of China has consistently resisted pressure for the establishment of any new SEZs. On the other hand, since 1984 it has sanctioned the establishment of an ever-growing number of economic zones. And in addition to those sanctioned by the central government, many provinces, cities, towns and even villages have established economic zones of their own, each offering incentives to industry to invest in them. By 1993 over 9,000 economic zones had been established

---

[2] To understand why it was felt necessary to restrict such activities to the SEZs, Westerners should consider a situation in which their government proposed to encourage experiments with a communist economic management system.

throughout China.[3] The process of zone proliferation has raised the question of the role such economic zones should play in the opening up and economic reform programme and whether the resources absorbed in their construction and maintenance are being used effectively. In particular, as the reform process continues, what continuing role in the vanguard, if any, is there for the SEZs to play?

The economic zones which have been established in the hope of emulating and extending the perceived success of the SEZs fall into several categories. There are Economic and Technological Development Zones, Hi-Tech Development Zones, Export Processing Zones, Free Trade Zones, a Financial Zone and Free Ports and specialized zones along the Yangtse river and along inland borders. In addition to the zones there are designated open cities, deltas, peninsulas and areas. The proliferation of titles has created some confusion as to the nature of the roles the different zones are supposed to play. The only common denominator is that they are all 'open areas', i.e. areas in which various specified direct economic links with foreigners are allowed, such links being prohibited to residents of other areas. The nature of the links permitted varies by type of zone, as does the nature of the encouragement given by the different levels of government in support of those links, although the SEZs remain the most liberal. (See Annex for a typology of zone types and the policies which apply to them.)

The 'Spring Wind' speeches of Deng Xiaoping early in 1992 focused national and international attention on China's five Special Economic Zones. After the events of 4 June 1989 critics of the SEZs had become more vocal, describing the zones as 'bastions of capitalism'.

---

[3] This is the figure given by the Ministry of Agriculture, which includes all proposed zones down to the village level. The State Land Administration gives the figure as 2,700, the then State Economic Planning Commission as 1,700 and the Special Economic Zones Office of the State Council as 1,800. The difference in the figures is probably due to differences in the level of public authority on which the data were collected – village, township, city, municipality or province. Figures from *Business Weekly,* as quoted in the *International Herald Tribune,* 8 February 1993. Subsequently many of these zones were closed down and currently there are no accurate figures on how many remain open.

Deng's intervention was a direct response to this criticism and was aimed at maintaining and increasing the pace of 'opening up and economic reform' in China by drawing attention to what he saw as the remarkable success story of the country's SEZs. He held them up as models for the rest of China to emulate. This position was taken up generally and the continuing importance of their role was stressed at the 14th Party Congress in 1992. In April 1993 Communist Party Chairman and President Jiang Zemin again stressed the importance of the SEZs and said that 'the special economic zones should continue to serve as national vanguards in reform and opening to the outside world'.[4] And again in 1995, at the Fifth Plenum of the 14th Party Congress, President Jiang and Premier Li Peng both reiterated that the basic policies towards the five SEZs (and Pudong New Zone, as it is now called) remained unchanged, although President Jiang did indicate that he thought the SEZs had become an issue in regional inequality.[5]

This paper investigates the role currently being played by SEZs in China. It further examines the relevance of that role to other locations in China and to other economies in transition. Chapter 2 provides a background for the analysis, discussing the origins of the SEZs and the evolution of the policies which apply in them. It also analyses the achievement of the SEZs in terms of their record on investment flows, trade growth and contributions to the domestic economy. Chapter 3 focuses on the role of the SEZs as economic policy laboratories and their significance in the national economic reform process. Chapter 4 provides an overall evaluation of the role of the SEZs and makes some policy recommendations.

---

[4] As reported in *China Daily*, 21 April 1993.

[5] Reported in *China News Analysis*, January 1996, p. 6.

# 2 BACKGROUND AND ACHIEVEMENTS

The initiative for the establishment of the first economic zone in China came from a Chinese-owned firm in Hong Kong, China Merchants Steam Navigation Company, which wished to expand its operations by taking advantage of low-cost land across the border in Bao'an County, developing an area from which it and other foreign investors could take advantage of the Chinese market and also expand export activities. Acceptance of the proposal by the State Council led to the establishment of the Shekou Industrial Zone in 1979. The area around Shekou was quickly established as a zone in which advantage could be taken of the proximity of Hong Kong. The new zone was Shenzhen, later to be established as a municipality with its own government. This expanded zone became the first SEZ in China, the Shenzhen Special Economic Zone. The second, in Zhuhai, the area contiguous with Macao, was also established in mid-1979, quickly followed by the third (also in Guangdong) at Shantou, which has a large and extensive expatriate community. The first outside Guangdong, at Xiamen in Fujian, was established in 1980. By the time the fifth SEZ, Hainan island, was established in 1988 there had been many other developments in the opening up policy.[6]

The apparent early successes of the SEZs led to a conceptual expansion from the model of Southeast Asian export processing zones to something more ambitious in terms of policies, activities and physical dimensions. As awareness of the developmental impact of foreign investment and market mechanisms grew, the scope of operation of the zones was extended. All five include farmland where investors have been invited to develop commercial agriculture. All five have also developed a tourism industry and a residential housing market aimed

---

[6] For a more extensive history of the establishment of the SEZs see Crane (1990).

primarily at overseas Chinese, especially compatriots in Taiwan, Macao and Hong Kong and residents of Singapore. All five have developed a significant tertiary sector which has grown, and continues to grow, in relative importance.

More importantly, what has always distinguished the Special Economic Zones as 'special' is their role as economic 'laboratories'. The SEZs are seen as areas within which the local authorities, under the guidance and overall control of the central government and subject to supervision by provincial governments, can encourage foreign investment and also domestic investment from hinterland authorities by allowing them to operate in a policy environment based much more on market mechanisms than is the case elsewhere in the economy. The effects of these experiments on foreign investment, foreign management techniques and foreign technology, and the general awareness of the developments they encourage in market economies, are to be watched by authorities and enterprises in the hinterland. By using the SEZs as 'windows' in this way the hinterland authorities and enterprises can decide which experiments it could be useful to move over the 'bridge' into the greater Chinese economy. In his 1992 'Spring Wind' speeches Deng Xiaoping reiterated that the function of the SEZs was to continue to carry out such experiments with market mechanisms and to be the windows and bridges for the hinterland to the outside world, and for the outside world into China. He also said that he had made a mistake in not extending SEZ treatment to Shanghai from the outset. This position is reflected in the fact that, apart from the SEZs, the Pudong development area of Shanghai is the only place which gives foreign-funded enterprises (FFEs) identical, or preferential, treatment and in which a specific new market mechanism experiment has been introduced into China, the experiment in question being the permission given to foreign companies to engage in trading activities, including retail trade.

The application of the opening up process has been extended to other areas. The first extension was to 14 coastal cities (later expanded to 15[7]), and then to whole coastal delta areas and peninsulas. This geo-

---

[7] Dalian, Qinhuangdao, Tianjin, Yantai, Qingdao, Lianyungang, Nantong, Shanghai, Ningbo, Wenzhou, Fuzhou, Guangzhou, Zhangjiang, Weihai and Behei.

**Table 2.1 : Extent and population, 1994**

|  | Shenzhen | Shantou | Zhuhai | Xiamen | Hainan |
|---|---|---|---|---|---|
| Original size (km²) | 327.5 | 1.6 | 6.81 | 2.5 | 34,000 |
| Current size | 327.5 | 234.0 | 123.0 | 130.0 | 34,000 |
| Population (million) | 3.355 | 1.030 | 1.015 | 1.200 | 7.114 |

*Note*: Data for population include adjacent counties under the jurisdiction of the zone authorities.

graphical expansion of the areas opened up has continued since 1979 without a break; in 1992 it was extended to the border areas with the former USSR and with Vietnam. However, despite this expansion, the 'special' nature of the SEZs continues, and this chapter concentrates on their particular economic achievement.

## The data[8]

*Size and location*

The original Special Economic Zone was Shekou Industrial Zone but, as we have seen, this was quickly incorporated into the larger Shenzhen Special Economic Zone, which continued to benefit from special privileges. The other two original zones in Guangdong Province also expanded in extent, as Table 2.1 shows. Similarly, the fourth SEZ, Xiamen in Fujian Province, was also expanded and now covers the whole of Xiamen island. Proposals are in hand for a further expansion of all four zones. The fifth SEZ, Hainan island, was part of Guangdong Province when it was set up in April 1988. Its status was raised to that of province at the same time.

---

[8] Almost all of the data relating to the Special Economic Zones used in this section are taken from the 1992 and 1995 Yearbooks of the individual zones, and were processed by the author with assistance from Wang Lina and Li Hai Yan. These yearbooks are the only source recognized by the Special Economic Zones Office of the State Council as being consistent and reliable. There is no published source of data covering all of the zones. The data from the Yearbooks are supplemented in some instances with details from the *China Statistical Yearbook 1995* and the *Almanac of China's Foreign Economic Relations and Trade, 1993/94.*

All five SEZs are large by comparison with typical export process-ing zones. Indeed, the whole of Hainan island was established as a SEZ but given the size of the island, 34,000km², the provincial government has followed a policy of establishing zones within the zone, some sim-ilar to an industrial estate, and others on a specialized basis such as the tourist development area at Sanya, the free trade area at Yangpu, and the Macao and Hong Kong Development Zone in Haikou. This 'zones within zones' approach has also been followed by the other SEZs, espe-cially the larger zones in Shenzhen and Xiamen.

The location of three of the original zones was determined by proximity to these Chinese communities, Shenzhen being contiguous to Hong Kong, Zhuhai to Macao, Xiamen the closest mainland town to Taiwan (and one with many links with the Taiwanese). Shantou was selected because of its extensive links with overseas Chinese commu-nities, particularly in Indonesia and Thailand. Hainan, too, is close to Hong Kong, but is also easily accessible from Taiwan and Singapore, and from Japan. All five SEZs are in the southeastern coastal area where the opening up and economic reform programme has been emphasized.

*Investment*

The bulk of the investment in the zones comes from within China. As Table 2.2 shows, investment in capital construction in the SEZs, includ-ing infrastructure, has been financed mainly from Chinese sources. This preponderance of domestic investment is characteristic of all five zones, but is particularly marked in the case of Hainan where, of 1,572 enter-prises established by the end of 1991, some 1,487 were Chinese-owned, mainly by state and municipal enterprises from the mainland. The dominance is not quite so marked when measured in terms of funds invested. Using a notional exchange rate of 8.3 yuan to the dol-lar, investment accounted for about 74 per cent of total, cumulative investment by the end of 1994, or 60 per cent if the dubious data for Xiamen are omitted.

Chinese state enterprises and collective enterprises are the domi-nant form of business in all five SEZs. The data on investment under-estimate the proportion of Chinese funds in the total, since in addition to the investment identified as domestic, there is some Chinese fund-

Table 2.2: Investment employed by the end of 1994 and numbers of firms established by the end of 1991

| | Shenzhen | Shantou | Zhuhai | Xiamen | Hainan | Total SEZ |
|---|---|---|---|---|---|---|
| Total investment in capital construction (end 1994, billion yuan) | 23.00 | 9.58 | 9.25 | 9.53 | 20.46 | 71.82 |
| Foreign funds employed[a] (end 1994, US$ billion) | 1.73 | 0.77 | 0.76 | 1.87 | 1.23 | 6.36 |
| Foreign funds employed as % of total investment, using 8.3 as exchange rate | 62 | 67 | 54 | 163[b] | 50 | 74 |
| Total number of industrial enterprises established by end 1991[c] of which: | 1,920 | 751 | 964 | 996 | 1,572 | 6,203 |
| Foreign-funded | 703 | n.a. | 348 | 368 | 85 | 1,504 |
| State and collective | 1,217 | 483 | 599 | 568 | 1,445 | 4,312 |
| Others[d] | 13 | 268 | 365 | 60 | 42 | 748 |

Notes:

[a]  Includes foreign bank loans.

[b]  Actual inflows of foreign capital exceeded total investment in Xiamen by the end of 1994.

[c]  Excludes village industries.

[d]  Includes domestic joint ventures, private enterprises and (in the case of Shantou) also foreign-funded enterprises.

**Table 2.3: Major sources of funds invested in capital construction (Y100m)**

|  | Shenzhen (1994) | Zhuhai (1991) | Xiamen (1994) | Hainan (1994) | China (1994) |
|---|---|---|---|---|---|
| State investment | 0.0 | 0.2 | 1.9 | 4.8 | 530 |
| Domestic loans | 31.7 | 2.5 | 17.3 | 51.9 | 3,703 |
| Foreign capital | 33.4 | 3.8 | 11.3 | 1.3 | 1,769 |
| Self-raised | 119.8 | 11.9 | 34.6 | 108.0 | 8,001 |
| Total | 184.9 | 18.4 | 65.1 | 166.0 | 14,003 |

ing in the figures for 'foreign funds used'. It is now accepted, but difficult to document, that some of the so-called foreign investment in joint-venture foreign-funded enterprises is actually derived from Chinese-owned enterprises abroad, especially in Hong Kong. Some of this is perfectly legal, such enterprises being well-established banks or other concerns which raise funds commercially on the Hong Kong capital and money markets. Some, however, are reputedly firms established abroad illegally with the purpose of building up foreign-exchange balances, partly with the intention of funding joint ventures in China in order to benefit from preferential treatment, especially in the form of lower taxes. It is difficult to quantify such flows, but their existence should be borne in mind when assessing the total. The other problem with data is that much of the 'investment' made by Chinese partners takes the form of bank loans, about one-third of their total investment in Shenzhen being financed in this way (see Table 2.3).

*Source of funds*

In recent years the biggest single share of the investment has come from 'self-raised' funds in the form of reinvested profits and from local government owners of state enterprises who have raised funds from locally imposed taxes, sales of land leases and profits from other activities. Data (Table 2.3) are available only for Shenzhen, Xiamen and Hainan for 1994 and for Zhuhai for 1991. For these four zones the ratio of self-raised finance to total investment (in 1994 for the first three zones and in 1991 for Zhuhai) was 65 per cent, 53 per cent and 65 per cent

**Table 2.4 Foreign funds employed 1991, their source and allocation by sector**

|  | Shenzhen | Shantou | Zhuhai | Xiamen | Hainan | China |
|---|---|---|---|---|---|---|
| Total (US$ bn) | 0.58 | n.a. | 0.17 | n.a. | 0.22 | 115.5 |
| of which from: |  |  |  |  |  |  |
|   Hong Kong | 0.32 |  | 0.58 |  | 0.123 | 29.2 |
|   Taiwan | 0.002 |  | 0.013 |  | 0.028 | 4.7 |
|   USA | 0.007 |  | — |  | 0.003 | 4.4 |
|   Japan | 0.14 |  | 0.035 |  | 0.052 | 18.9 |
|   Macao | — |  | 0.056 |  | — | — |
|  |  |  |  |  |  |  |
| and by sector, to: |  |  |  |  |  |  |
|   Agriculture | — |  | — |  | 0.015 | n.a. |
|   Industry | 0.35 |  | 0.143 |  | 0.064 | n.a. |
|   Trade | 0.008 |  | — |  | 0.054 | n.a. |
|   Communications | 0.009 |  | — |  | 0.014 | n.a. |
|   Property | 0.11 |  | 0.019 |  | 0.06 | n.a. |
|   Finance and insurance | 0.098 |  | — |  | — | n.a. |
| No of contracts approved | 734 | 273 | 536 | 213 | 476 | 25,703 |
| of which, from: |  |  |  |  |  |  |
|   Hong Kong | 642 | n.a. | 279 | 90 | 292 | n.a |
|   Taiwan | 32 | n.a. | 35 | 90 | 89 | n.a |
|   Japan | 17 | n.a. | 10 | n.a. | 14 | n.a |
|   USA | 18 | n.a. | 11 | n.a. | 21 | n.a |
|   Singapore | 8 | n.a. | 5 | n.a. | 17 | n.a |
|   Macao | 0 | n.a. | 181 | n.a. | 0 | n.a |

respectively of the three main sources of finance and 65 per cent in Zhuhai. Support from the central and provincial governments was limited to the early years, although with a still much lower tax and banking base, Hainan continues to depend for a significant part of its investment on subventions from the centre, through the planning system. Funding for infrastructure development – particularly in Hainan – has also been obtained from the international financial institutions and bilateral donors, although details are not available.

Table 2.3 also shows that in the three zones for which data are available, investment in the industry sector and in the communications and telecommunications and property and public utilities sectors combined is roughly the same. This contrasts with the rest of the economy where investment in industry is roughly two-and-a-half times as large as in the other two sectors combined.

Detailed data on the foreign sources of funds used in the zones are only available for 1991. The most important source of foreign funds in the SEZs (whether investment is direct or indirect) is Hong Kong. Firms from other locations, particularly from countries which do not have diplomatic relations with China (including Korea in 1991), invest in China via intermediary firms in Hong Kong. Many of these firms are small enterprises. This is reflected in the fact that they account for a larger share of the numbers of enterprises investing in the zones than they do of foreign funds utilized there. For example, Hong Kong firms accounted for 642, or 87 per cent, of the foreign investment proposals approved in Shenzhen in 1991, but for only US$320 million, or 55 per cent, of the US$580 million invested in that year. Taiwan is the second most important source of foreign funds in all zones except Zhuhai, where Macao comes second. In Xiamen Taiwan is equally important as a source of foreign funds as Hong Kong. Japan, too, plays an increasingly important role. By 1991 it accounted for almost a quarter of the foreign funds invested in Shenzhen, 21 per cent in Zhuhai and 24 per cent in Hainan. On the other hand, it accounted for only 2 per cent of the total number of investment proposals approved in Shenzhen and Zhuhai in that year and for only 3 per cent in Hainan: Japanese investments tend to be much larger than those from Taiwan and Hong Kong.

Most Hong Kong and Taiwanese investment is in processing and assembly industries, and this is reflected in Table 2.4, where industry is shown to be the main target of foreign funds. In Hainan investment in trading companies is almost as important as that in industry; although with the recent shift of emphasis towards the tourism sector, the relative share of real estate has grown since 1991.

Table 2.5 shows that wholly foreign-owned foreign-funded enterprises (FFEs) have become a significant factor in the opening up process. In the early years there were very few such enterprises, partly because of an unwillingness on the Chinese side to accept them and partly due to caution on the part of foreign investors. They now account for a significant share of total investment. In 1991 half or more

**Table 2.5: Foreign direct investment by type of enterprise, 1994 (US$m)**

| | Shenzhen | Shantou | Zhuhai | Xiamen | Hainan[a] | Total SEZ |
|---|---|---|---|---|---|---|
| (1) Total funds employed of which: | 628 | 695 | 441 | 2,434 | 451 | 4,649 |
| (2) Joint ventures | 384 | 112 | 175 | 888 | 111 | 1,670 |
| (3) Cooperative ventures | 84 | 381 | 106 | 686 | 87 | 1,344 |
| (4) Wholly foreign-owned | 159 | 203 | 160 | 860 | 253 | 1,635 |
| (4) as % of (1) | 25 | 29 | 36 | 35 | 56 | 35 |

[a] The data for Hainan are unreliable.

of all foreign direct investment (note that data in Table 2.4 include foreign loans) in Shantou, Zhuhai, and Hainan went into wholly foreign-owned enterprises.

*Sectoral disposition*

No data are available on the sectoral distribution of realized investment. The only sectoral data available relate to the distribution by sector of foreign investment approvals (Table 2.6). These show that the manufacturing sector is still the main destination of foreign investment. In Shenzhen and Zhuhai this accounted for more than two-thirds of the total. In Hainan and Xiamen, in both of which tourism is a significant sector, it was 48 per cent and 43 per cent respectively.

*Use of funds*

Contrary to the hopes of central and local governments, there is no evidence of significant amounts of investment in high-tech industry in the manufacturing sector. There are no data which allow us to categorize firms scientifically by level of technology, but the large proportion of firms involved in simple processing and assembling activities or simple labour-intensive production, or predominantly involved in trading activities, suggests that low-tech production is dominant. Many high-tech products are manufactured in the zones, sometimes with high-tech

## Table 2.6: Sectoral allocation of foreign investment approvals (US$m)[a]

|  | Shenzhen (1991) | Shantou[b] (1992) | Zhuhai (1991) | Xiamen (1994) | Hainan (1994) |
|---|---|---|---|---|---|
| Primary sector[c] | 8.9 | 19 | 1.6 | 10.50 | 22.2 |
| Manufacturing | 778.0 | 666 | 372.0 | 886.0 | 837.0 |
| Construction | 38.4 | — | 27.5 | 17.1 | 57.0 |
| Communications | 16.7 | 9 | 6.1 | 0 | 0 |
| Trade and catering | 57.4 | 12 | 6.4 | 317.0 | 71.3 |
| Housing and public utilities | 172.0 | 135 | 116.0 | 601.0 | 933.0 |
| Others | 80.7 | 2 | 7.8 | 6.9 | 7.4 |
| Totals of above | 1,152.1 | 158 | 537.4 | 1,838.5 | 1,927.9 |

*Notes*:
[a] Does not include investment by Chinese partner.
[b] Data in this column are for number of investments.
[c] Agriculture, forestry, husbandry and fishery.

equipment, but the actual processes carried out are only low-tech ones. Many enterprises are simply 'screwdriver' factories. A factory in Xiamen 'producing' state-of-the-art video recorders is a good example. All the inputs are imported, including the labelling and packaging (which is carefully designed to suggest that the recorders are imported as finished items), and the only processes which take place in the factory are assembly, testing and packaging. The imported testing equipment is high-tech.

*Production*

Table 2.7 shows the results of the investment. Gross output in the zones has increased rapidly. The growth rates remain high, and the gross output of the zones has been increasing faster than the national average. This was 11 per cent for the year 1990–91, while in Shenzhen the growth rate was 29 per cent, in Shantou 27 per cent, in Zhuhai 54 per cent and in Xiamen 23 per cent. Even in Hainan, which became an SEZ only in 1988 and in which early investment has been concentrated on economic and social infrastructure, the rate for 1990–91 was 14 per cent. The growth in output of the four mainland zones since 1980

**Table 2.7: Output (GNP) in the zones (billion yuan, current prices)**

|  | Shenzhen | Shantou | Zhuhai | Xiamen | Hainan | China |
|---|---|---|---|---|---|---|
| GNP 1980 | 0.27 | 0.16 | 0.24 | 0.64 | n.a. | 447.0 |
| GNP 1990 | 13.5 | 2.92 | 3.17 | 5.05 | 9.5 | 1,785.5 |
| GNP 1991 | 17.4 | 3.72 | 4.87 | 6.22 | 10.8 | 1,985.5 |
| of which: |  |  |  |  |  |  |
| Primary | 0.8 | 0.23 | 0.35 | 0.64 | 5.02 | 528.9 |
| Secondary | 10.5 | 2.15 | 2.23 | 3.34 | 2.46 | 914.7 |
| Tertiary | 6.1 | 1.34 | 2.28 | 2.23 | 3.31 | 540.5 |
| GDP 1994 | 63.82 | 28.32 | 23.01 | 24.60 | 35.97 |  |
| of which industry | 56.00 | 19.50 | 18.00 | 18.90 | 11.79 |  |

Note. The area covered by some zones changed during the period. see Table 2.1.

is several times the national average. The substantial increases in output between 1991 and 1994 suggested by the figures are partly explained by the significant inflation over that period and partly by faster than average growth.

*Foreign trade*

Table 2.8 shows that the zones have seen a remarkable growth in exports since their foundation. The most rapid rises have occurred most recently, as foreign investment has grown and matured, although Shenzhen saw an unusual slowdown in 1990–91 (and has picked up again since). Table 2.7 also shows that FFEs now play a major role in the export performance of the SEZs, except in Hainan where trade is still dominated by Foreign Trade Corporations (FTCs) owned by the zone authorities themselves. The picture is somewhat confused, however, by the fact that some of the FFEs are joint ventures partly owned by FTCs.

*Destination of exports*

As Table 2.9 shows, Hong Kong is by far the most important destination for the exports of the two Special Economic Zones. This reflects

**Table 2.8: Exports from SEZs**

|  | Shenzhen | Shantou | Zhuhai | Xiamen | Hainan | China |
|---|---|---|---|---|---|---|
| Value US$ bn |  |  |  |  |  |  |
| Current prices |  |  |  |  |  |  |
| 1981 | 0.2 | neg. | 0.1 | 1.4 | 0.5 | 220 |
| 1990 | 50.5 | 5.7 | 8.1 | 9.2 | 5.4 | 621 |
| 1991 | 56.0 | 8.2 | 11.1 | 12.7 | 6.7 | 719 |
| 1994 | 183.6 | 25.9 | 19.9 | 31.2 | 9.5 | n.a. |
|  |  |  |  |  |  |  |
| Exports by FFEs |  |  |  |  |  |  |
| (US$ bn, 1991) | 29.0 | 2.8 | 5.0 | 3.0 | 0.5 | 120.5 |
| As % of total 1991 | 51.7 | 34.5 | 45.6 | 24.0 | 8.5 | 16.8 |
|  |  |  |  |  |  |  |
| Exports by municipal |  |  |  |  |  |  |
| FTC (US$ bn 1991) | 9.7 | n.a. | 3.3 | 6.2 | 4.6 | n.a. |
| As % of total 1991 | 17.4 |  | 41.0 | 50.0 | 73.0 |  |
|  |  |  |  |  |  |  |
| Exports by hinterland |  |  |  |  |  |  |
| FTC (US$ bn) | 1.8 | n.a. | n.a. | 2.2 | n.a. | n.a. |
| As % of 1991 | 3.3 |  |  | 17.5 |  |  |

*Note*: No comparable breakdown of data is available for all zones for 1994, but figures for Hainan and Shenzhen show the same patterns as 1991, i.e. municipal trading corporations continue to dominate in Hainan (79%) and foreign-funded enterprises continue to be the main traders in Shenzhen (29%).

the heavy investment by Hong Kong-based companies. Much of this trade is entrepôt trade, being re-exported from Hong Kong, but lack of data makes it impossible to put a reliable estimate on this. Japan is the second most important destination for exports from the SEZs, though a long way behind, followed by the USA (which is also thought to be the destination of many of the goods first exported from the SEZs to Hong Kong) and then Germany and Singapore. These five countries represent the top five destinations for all of the SEZs except Zhuhai, where Germany and Singapore give way to Macao and Thailand.

When interpreting SEZ trade data it should be borne in mind that they include not only exports produced in the zones but also exports made on behalf of inland provinces on an agency basis. The data on this trade are difficult to come by, but figures available suggest that almost

**Table 2.9: First destination of exports from SEZs, 1992 (US$m)**

|  | Shenzhen | Zhuhai | Shantou | Xiamen | Hainan | Total for SEZs | China |
|---|---|---|---|---|---|---|---|
| Hong Kong | 4,343 | 234 | 874 | 421 | 482 | 6,354 | 37,512 |
| Japan | 73 | 19 | 39 | 164 | 53 | 348 | 11,678 |
| USA | 143 | 6 | 41 | 80 | 18 | 288 | 8,593 |
| Germany | 15 |  | 12 | 67 | 20 | 99 | 2,448 |
| Singapore | 36 |  | 29 | 34 | 16 | 79 | 2,030 |
| South Korea |  |  |  | 51 |  | 51 | 2,405 |
| Macao |  | 19 |  |  |  | 19 | 529 |
| Thailand |  | 5 | 4 |  | 13 | 13 | 895 |

**Table 2.10: Processing trade 1991 (US$m)**

|  | Shenzhen | Shantou | Zhuhai | Xiamen | Hainan | China |
|---|---|---|---|---|---|---|
| Total exports of which: | 560.0 | 80.2 | 110.1 | 120.7 | 60.7 | 7190 |
| Processing trade | 150.3 | 7 | 20.5 | 8.3 | 4 | 1090 |
| Share of exports made in SEZ (%) | 70.0 | n.a. | n.a. | 57.9 | n.a. | n.a. |

30 per cent of the exports of Shenzhen comprise such agency trade, while the figure for Xiamen may be even higher at 40 per cent. This is important when trying to assess the balance-of-payments position of the zones. Similarly, it needs to be remembered that much of the export trade of the SEZs is in processed and assembled goods. The trade data show only domestic value added if such trade is subject to a formal and registered processing trade agreement, otherwise they are entered in gross terms. Table 2.10 shows that the national average for such registered trade was 15 per cent in 1991, the latest year for which comparable data are available. The figure was higher in Shenzhen (at 27 per cent) and Zhuhai (23 per cent), demonstrating the importance of easy cross-border communications for such trade.

**Table 2.11: Balance of trade data (US$bn)**

|  | Shenzhen | Shantou | Zhuhai | Xiamen | Hainan |
|---|---|---|---|---|---|
| Exports 1990 | 5.1 | 0.57 | 0.80 | 0.92 | 0.54 |
| Imports 1990 | 4.5 | 0.73 | 0.89 | 0.78 | 0.44 |
| Exports 1994 | 18.36 | 2.59 | 1.99 | 3.12 | 0.95 |
| Imports 1994 | 16.84 | 2.37 | 2.31 | 2.57 | 1.81 |

*Balance of payments*

In terms of national objectives, however, what matters is not growth rates of trade, but the net balance of payments generated by the international activities of the zones. Accurate balance-of-payments data for the Special Economic Zones cannot be obtained, since payments data other than those for trade are not collected on a zone basis, nor are capital movements data, and also because there is widespread smuggling and, reportedly, widespread over- and under-invoicing. Such official trade data as there are (Table 2.11) suggest that only Shenzhen and Xiamen had a trade surplus in 1991, though it should be noted that some of the imports are one-off capital goods imports. In the case of Hainan, the surplus in 1990 turned into a substantial deficit in 1994.

*Employment*

The contribution of the Special Economic Zones to the overall employment situation in China in minimal. Table 2.12 shows that total employment in industry and the tertiary sector in all five zones was only around 2.5 million. Some of this is accounted for by enterprises catering to the needs of the local population, and some simply represents shifts of jobs from the hinterland in enterprises attracted by the incentives available in the Special Economic Zones. Estimates which are mentioned from time to time suggest that firms based in Hong Kong alone employ more than 5 million workers in factories outside the zones.

The data in Table 2.12 also suggest a wide variation in labour productivity between the zones in 1991. Taking the output data from

**Table 2.12: Employment in the SEZs, 1991 (10,000)**

|  | Shenzhen | Shantou | Zhuhai | Xiamen | Hainan |
|---|---|---|---|---|---|
| **1991** | | | | | |
| Population (million) | 119.0 | 87.3 | 22.1 | 39.8 | 661.0 |
| Labour force | 68.0 | 51.7 | 19.0 | n.a. | 316.0 |
| of which: | | | | | |
| Agriculture | 1.05 | 22.5 | 2.5 | 1.3 | 217.6 |
| Industry | 41.0 | 21.8 | n.a. | 18.1 | 31.7 |
| Tertiary | 25.0 | 29.6 | n.a. | 13.2 | 66.7 |
| **1994** | | | | | |
| Population (million) | 335 | 103 | 102 | 120 | 711 |
| Labour force | 223 | | | | 335 |
| of which: | | | | | |
| Agriculture | 5 | | | | 204 |
| Industry | 153 | | | | 40 |
| Tertiary | 65 | | | | 91 |

Table 2.7, output per worker in industry in Shenzhen was around 25,600 yuan in 1991 and in Xiamen 18,500 yuan, while in Shantou it was only 9,900 yuan and in Hainan as little as 7,800 yuan. By 1994 output per worker had increased to 28,619 yuan in Shenzhen and 10,737 yuan in Hainan; in both cases this represents a fall in productivity after inflation is allowed for.

# 3 THE EXPERIMENTS

## Introduction

Not all of the policy initiatives which constitute the 'opening up and economic reform' programme began as experiments in the SEZs. Many reform measures have been introduced on a country-wide basis, for example the 'household responsibility system' in agriculture, price reforms, reforms in the management of state enterprises, the development of free commodity markets, the establishment of a private sector, and the decentralization of the management of foreign trade. This chapter addresses only those reforms which began as experiments in the zones; other policy reforms are referred to only in so far as they have affected developments there. Some of the experiments represent the removal of obstacles which prohibit, or used to prohibit, certain activities in China, for example the establishment of foreign-funded enterprises. Some involved the introduction of incentives to encourage certain sorts of activity. They can be categorized as those which relate to the characteristics of the economic management system itself and those which relate to specific factor markets. The two types are outlined below.

## System experiments

### SEZs as experiments with the economic management system

The establishment of economic zones represents acceptance by a government that there are some economic objectives which it cannot achieve by relying on the domestic economic policy framework. Thus the very existence of zones represents a major experiment in the reform of Chinese economic policy. Initially at least, the model was the export processing zones of South Korea, Taiwan and other Asian countries with successful export records. As their name implies, export processing zones have a single function: the development of exports, in order to generate foreign-exchange inflows and create employment opportunities. Companies investing in them benefit from incentives under various policies which are not available to companies elsewhere in the country.[9] They are usually relatively small in area, do not include residential areas and have management powers delegated to them which give them a high degree of autonomy, especially with respect to the treatment of investment applications.

By contrast, China's Special Economic Zones cover large areas, including agricultural as well as industrial districts. They are run by local governments which have to carry the full range of local government responsibilities at the municipal level (except in the case of Hainan which is a province), as well as running the SEZs. The single-objective approach of export processing zones was quickly dropped in favour of a multi-objective strategy. This was in part a recognition of the fact that China could not at that time attract investment from the sort of firms which had been responsible for the successful development of export processing zones in other countries. It was believed that to attract firms other than those solely interested in labour-intensive processing activities, China would have to trade access to its domestic market for inflows of capital, managerial skills, technology and access to international markets. It was also quickly discovered that there was a vast pent-up demand among overseas Chinese, especially in Hong Kong and Taiwan, for holidays and property in China. The zones, especially Shenzhen and Xiamen and later Hainan, were quickly geared up to meet this demand.

*Extra-plan investment*

Perhaps the most important factor differentiating the SEZs from other areas of China is that investment decisions taken there are to some extent outside the State Plan. As long as they can raise the extra funds from taxation, from profits made by enterprises they own (wholly or partially) or from banks in the zones, the local governments involved can establish their own infrastructure development and commercial

---

[9] Note that export processing zone policies can be applied on a factory-by-factory basis, as in Mauritius and Malaysia.

investment plans.[10] And enterprises in the zones, including state enterprises owned locally or by hinterland authorities, joint ventures and wholly foreign-owned firms, can make their own investment, production and marketing decisions. This gives the local authorities and state enterprises involved much more autonomy and flexibility than their counterparts elsewhere in the economy and is a major factor in attracting hinterland investment into the zones. The SEZ authorities have the power, within limits, to approve investment proposals, although this right has been extended to other authorities covered by the open coastal city and area policy.

## Preferential tax treatment

Foreign-funded enterprises in the other economic zones, such as Economic and Technological Development Zones (ETDZs), now receive the same tax treatment as FFEs investing in the SEZs. The corporation tax rate to which FFEs outside the zones are liable is 33 per cent. The rate in the zones is set at 15 per cent. This is the rate which obtained in Hong Kong at the time the policy was formulated – the aim being not to impose a tax disadvantage on SEZ investors compared with investors in Hong Kong, while not giving away tax revenue unnecessarily. The tax holiday of '2 plus 3' – i.e., the first two years in profit are tax-free and for the next three the tax rate is only 7.5 per cent – is also available to FFEs in all zones anywhere in China. There are various special rates depending on the type of activity: for example, if after the expiration of the tax holiday a firm is exporting more than 70 per cent of its output then the tax rate is only 10 per cent.

With respect to tax incentives, of far more significance than the treatment of FFEs is the incentive given to Chinese state enterprises.[11]

---

[10] In practice, where capital is not a binding constraint, other authorities, in particular the governments of Guangzhou and Guangdong, have taken on this role of approving extra-Plan investments, although they do not have this right *de jure*. As part of a package of reforms to be introduced in 1996, 75 per cent of tax revenues are to be remitted to the central government (as reported in the *China Daily Business Weekly*, 24–30 September 1995, p. 1).

[11] For a general discussion of tax treatment of FFEs in China see Khan (1991).

In the SEZs (and the ETDZs) they also pay only 15 per cent compared with 55 per cent elsewhere (this was reduced to 33 per cent for most enterprises at the end of 1993[12]). They still had to remit a share of their profits, if any, to their 'owners'. In the case of Xiamen, for example, this negotiable 'dividend' is set at a rate which often gives the Xiamen municipal government a total combined return of tax and dividends of approximately 55 per cent (the actual rate depending on the performance of the company). The lower tax rate means that for hinterland owners of state enterprises there is a substantial incentive to invest in the zones. In an attempt to counter this, many hinterland governments, on various levels, have introduced matching tax concessions for investors in the development zones which they have established. Although not centrally approved, such tax concessions can be provided as a result of the tendency towards tax farming within the Chinese fiscal system.

As part of a package of reforms being discussed early in 1996 these tax privileges would be removed in the near future as the tax treatment of enterprises in the SEZs is brought into line with those operating elsewhere in the economy. Although the government has been fairly definite in its statements of intention, for example at the Fifth Plenum, there had been no formal announcement at the time of writing.

*Trade policy*

Since the establishment of the SEZs, firms investing there (FFEs automatically and Chinese state enterprises after approval) have been exempted from import licences. This exemption covers capital goods specified in the investment plan, and intermediate goods and raw materials needed in production. Duty-free imports of intermediate goods and raw materials are subject to approval by the customs service, usually via the registration of an import plan on a six-monthly basis. The

---

[12] The 33 per cent rate also replaced the varying rates of between 10 and 50 per cent to which small state enterprises, collectives and private-sector enterprise were liable. See 'Tax reforms must set a new unified standard', *China Daily*, 3 September 1993, p. 4. This article also states that the average negotiated tax rate for large state enterprises was less than 40 per cent, plus an average of 34 per cent of profits.

SEZs are treated as separate customs areas and in addition to being free of import licensing these approved imports also enter duty free. If the products of enterprises in the SEZs are exported they are free of all duties and indirect taxes. In addition, duty-free items are exempted from all indirect internal taxes. If firms import items which are sold in the zones with or without further processing then they are liable to pay only 50 per cent of the full duty and indirect tax rates, except for cars, motor-bikes and television sets and other durable consumer goods, on which the full duty and excise taxes are supposed be paid. If firms in the zones sell their products on to the Chinese hinterland market, after having obtained approval as import substitution enterprises, they pay full tariffs and indirect taxes. The concessions were later extended to enterprises in the State Council-approved ETDZs and Science Parks, but not to the Open Coastal Cities. There is no exemption or reduction in duty or taxes for imports or output sold in the ETDZs as they are not separate customs areas.

The duty-free treatment of imports of capital goods by all enterprises in the SEZs was abolished as from 1 January 1996, with a grace period of three months for small companies and up to two years for larger companies. Duty-free concessions for intermediate goods, including cars, were also removed. Concessions for imports for raw materials to be used in exports remain, although monitoring to ensure that they are so used will be tightened to prevent abuses.

The *ex post* collection of duties and indirect taxes on sales in the SEZs and to the hinterland parallels the practice in most EPZs around the world. However, in other countries there is either tight control by the customs service on imports of raw materials and intermediate goods held in bond in the factories, or strict control by a customs-policed perimeter fence around the zone. Only Shenzhen operates such a fence, the 'second management line'. All other zones operate on a basis of trust plus occasional random checks. Firms are required to report sales to the zones or hinterland; private individuals are free to carry their purchases out of the zones without further payment of duties or taxes. Hainan, being an island, has a natural barrier, although it is not strictly policed. The other three hinterland zones operate tight surveillance over stocks of imported raw materials and intermediate goods held in bond. In Shenzhen and Hainan, and to a lesser extent in the other SEZs, sales by duty-free shops to hinterland residents, who take their purchases home duty free, make an increasingly important contribution to the local economy. In 1993 the tariff revenue collection system was changed radically, tariff rates and any exemptions being established and tariffs being collected at the time of entry instead of being settled at the end of the year.[13]

A new development is the establishment of free trade zones (also known as bonded zones). The first to be approved by the State Council was the Waigaoqiao Free Trade Area in Pudong in East Shanghai. This was not formally opened until early 1993, although it began operations early in 1992. In Waigaoqiao FFEs can also, uniquely in China, engage in trading activities (excluding retail trade). Two free trade zones in Shenzhen were approved later than Waigaoqiao but began operating earlier. The first to open was the Shataojiao Processing Zone in 1991. A new one, the Futian Free Trade Area, with a bridge directly into Hong Kong, commenced operations in 1993. There are other privileges for firms operating in these subzones. For example, they can recruit their labour direct without reference to the Labour Bureau. This free trade area initiative was quickly copied in the hinterland, and a bonded zone with equivalent privileges was set up in Tianjin in 1991. By 1993 thirteen free trade areas had been established with the approval of the State Council. In addition to the four already mentioned, zones were opened in Shantou, Xiamen, Haikou (Hainan), Dalian, Qingdao, Zhangjiagang (Jiangsu Province), Ningbo, Fuzhou and Guangzhou.

*Foreign exchange mechanism*

One of the first and most important of the policy experiments introduced in the SEZs was the establishment of foreign exchange swap centres.

Originally, all enterprises in the SEZs could retain 100 per cent of their export earnings. By 1985, this rate also applied to firms in development zones in Hainan (before it became an SEZ). Enterprises in Tibet were also allowed to retain their total foreign exchange earnings.

---

[13] *China Daily*, 4 September 1993.

FFEs which were allowed to sell in the domestic market, however, originally had no facility to obtain foreign exchange unless they were one of the few with State Plan allocations. On the other hand, some of those with total retention needed to sell foreign exchange rights in order to obtain Chinese currency for their local costs, although they were reluctant to do so at official rates. The foreign exchange adjustment centre (FEAC), or 'swap' centre, established in Shenzhen in 1985, was intended to allow these two types of company to balance, or swap, their foreign exchange market requirements at a mutually agreeable rate. The range of entities allowed to operate in the market increased and the sums involved grew in size as retention rights were extended. The number of swap centres was increased to meet the rise in demand and at its peak approached 100, although they were not networked and rates could vary from centre to centre.

The multiplicity of retention rights was reduced in 1993 to one principal rate which applied to most foreign exchange earning entities throughout China. Apart from oil and coal exporters, exporters of machinery and electronics products, the People's Liberation Army, all FFEs and all enterprises in Tibet, a retention rate of 80 per cent applied. The government retained the right to lower this to 50 per cent (paying for the additional 30 per cent at the swap market rate). Enterprises engaged in processing activities could retain 90 per cent of new foreign exchange earnings. Of the standard retention rate of 80 per cent, 10 per cent was allocated to the relevant local government, 10 per cent to the producing enterprises and 60 per cent to the foreign trade corporation (or the enterprise itself if it was one with direct trading rights). When the government exercised its right to lower the rate to 50 per cent, the 10 per cent was removed from the enterprise and 20 per cent from the FTCs.

Domestic firms still had to sell all their foreign exchange earnings to the Bank of China[14]: 20 per cent was sold at the official rate and 80 per cent in return for retention quota certificates which confer the right to repurchase foreign exchange at the official rate. These certifi-

---

[14] Except for firms in a few locations where an experiment with a cash retention system was tried out.

cates could be sold in the swap market. (Firms could also be allocated foreign exchange at the official rate through the national plan.) Foreign-funded enterprises had a 100 per cent retention rate and could maintain foreign exchange bank accounts. Thus what started as an experiment for foreign-funded enterprises in one SEZ crossed the bridge into the hinterland and became a nationally established mechanism with no remaining preferential treatment for enterprises in the SEZs.[15]

The whole retention scheme was abolished on 1 January 1994. Since then all enterprises throughout China have been treated alike, although at the time of writing foreign-funded enterprises must still operate through the swap centres while domestic enterprises have to sell all their foreign exchange earnings to banks and buy foreign exchange back as and when they require it – and can prove legitimate need.

As far as the foreign exchange market is concerned, the only remaining advantage for firms in the SEZs (and Pudong) is easier access to foreign banks, including in the case of Xiamen access to a foreign-funded, joint-venture bank which can also deal, within limits, in local currency. In the case of Shenzhen, firms may also benefit from the unique situation there that a foreign currency, the Hong Kong dollar, is a major component of the money supply and plays an important role in day-to-day business. Apart from the establishment of foreign banks, which is beginning to take place in the hinterland, these experiments – joint-venture banks and the local use of foreign currency – are unlikely to spread inland in the near future.

*Nature of enterprises*

With respect to enterprises, the main feature of the policy experiment in the SEZs relates to the extent of the forms of multi-ownership allowed there. Although the three forms of foreign-funded enterprise (wholly foreign-owned, joint venture, and cooperation agreement), private enterprises, state enterprises and collectives are now found throughout China, the ratio of wholly publicly owned firms is much

---

[15] For a full account of the 1992 retention system, see World Bank (1993), p. 28.

lower in the SEZs than in the hinterland. This is true even in Xiamen, where there are a large number of state enterprises which predate the formation of the SEZ. Chinese private enterprises are, subject to some restrictions, free to establish in any sector, anywhere, although owing to limited access to capital they are mainly confined to restaurants and other retail outlets. It is possible, however, that some collective enterprises are really private enterprises registering as collectives for tax reasons.

The growth of the joint-stock sector has also progressed faster in the zones than elsewhere. Foreign ownership participation through the medium of B shares (in which only foreign institutions can deal and for which settlement has to be in foreign exchange) has been taken further in Shenzhen than anywhere else, although in the spring of 1992 the first B share was quoted on the Shanghai exchange. By September 1993, 18 B shares were listed in Shenzhen and 11 in Shanghai, and Chinese companies had been listed on the Hong Kong and New York stock exchanges. Similarly, although branches of foreign banks are now found elsewhere in China, having been first introduced via the SEZs, the only joint-venture bank in the country – the Xiamen International Bank – is located in the Xiamen Special Economic Zone.

## Visas

One experiment still restricted to three of the SEZs is the more relaxed procedure for issuing visas for entry into China. For entry to Hainan, Shenzhen and Zhuhai, foreigners and residents of Taiwan and Hong Kong require no visas at all prior to arrival. Hainan can issue visas for up to 15 days at the port of arrival and these can be extended for a further two weeks without difficulty or delay. Shenzhen border authorities can issue visas for five days and Zhuhai authorities for three. In all three, standard visas can be issued when leaving for the mainland. In all five SEZs investors in FFEs and their expatriate management staff can be granted multiple entry visas. It is proposed to extend the practice of issuing multiple entry visas to Waigaoqiao Free Trade Zone in Pudong. Though seemingly a small matter in itself, this can be an important psychological factor, as obtaining visas abroad can be a time-consuming, frustrating and expensive process.

*Delegated government authority*

The four mainland SEZs are governed by their own local governments, each having responsibility for neighbouring areas as well. The original, more direct, responsibility of the provincial governments of Guangdong and Fujian has been devolved to the municipal level with their associated Peoples' Congresses. Hainan was established as a province, being separated from Guangdong soon after its establishment as an SEZ, in 1988. In principle the governments of the zones have a great deal of delegated power. However, the operation of that power is subject in many ways to influence and control from the central government, and, in the case of the four mainland zones, also from the provincial governments.

At an early stage powers to approve investment in the zones were devolved to their governments, although this was true for provincial and municipal governments too. Currently the zone governments can approve investments by Chinese companies up to limits of 100 million yuan for non-productive investment (such as hotels), 50 million for heavy industry and 30 million for light industry. Above these limits central government approval is required, from the State Planning Commission. Approval is also required from the central Ministry of Foreign Trade and Economic Cooperation (MOFTEC) if the investment involves imports or exports of any items covered by quotas or licences.

The SEZs have considerable freedom of manoeuvre in the area of taxation. The rates set by the central government appear to be maxima and the local governments running the SEZs seem to have the flexibility to set different rates and apply different exemptions and reductions on a firm-by-firm basis. The only constraint is apparently the need to raise revenue for its own purposes and to make any remittances to provincial and central levels of government, although even here there appears to be some flexibility as Shenzhen had not, as of 1993, remitted any tax revenues to the central government for three years. Hainan, as a backward area, does not remit any revenue to the central government but is a net recipient of fiscal transfers. Both Hainan and Shenzhen have adopted a value-added tax (VAT) on an experimental basis to replace other indirect taxes. This experiment was extended to the whole country at the beginning of 1994.

Dependence on the central government for transfers limits the independence of any authority. For instance, Hainan has been trying to reduce the size of its government, using the slogan 'small government, large society'. It cut the number of government departments to 27, about one-third of the number of departments and bureaux in the central government. However, central government departments and bureaux which did not have direct counterparts in Hainan began to make difficulties, including refusing to pass on grants on the grounds that without specialized offices there was no way of ensuring that the grants would be used for the purposes for which they were given. As a result, the structure of the government of Hainan has been returned to something approaching its former composition.

In principle two SEZs, Shenzhen and Hainan, have the right to legislate the enactment of rules and regulations for governing the practices of economic agents in their zones. But this freedom is severely curtailed by the 'grandfather clause' that any such rules and regulations have to be consistent with the central government legislation or position, as interpreted by the bureaucracy of the central government. For example, two 'approved' stock exchanges now exist, although for a long time there were no centrally established detailed rules and regulations for the day-to-day operation of such exchanges. Until 1993, the local branches of the People's Bank of China in Shenzhen and Shanghai 'regulated' the two exchanges but had no centrally established regulations to enforce; the operations of the exchanges were governed by rules and regulations devised by the local governments. Such central regulations were introduced in 1993 by the new national Securities Regulatory Commission, one of whose officials was appointed as the chief executive of the Shenzhen Stock Exchange in July 1993.[16]

Although there is no central government law preventing the establishment of stock exchanges, the initiative of the provincial government of Hainan in setting one up early in 1992 ran into strong resistance from the centre, forcing its closure. The Chinese principle of a strong central government working with local governments and peoples' congresses to modify central policies to suit local conditions is being severely tested in

---

[16] As reported in the *South China Morning Post*, 28 July 1993.

the case of SEZ governments which are supposed to be the pioneers of economic experimentation. The three largest SEZs, Hainan, Shenzhen and Xiamen, are now pressing for more genuine autonomy by being allowed to convert themselves into free ports, following the call by Deng Xiaoping to establish several 'socialist Hong Kongs' in China. These moves are being resisted by the central authorities.

On a different level, but related to the delegation of powers issue, is the issue of 'zones within the zones'. Although the Shekou Industrial Zone was incorporated into Shenzhen Special Economic Zone soon after its establishment it kept its status – equivalent to that of a county – until the end of its first ten-year lease. Even now, it has kept many of the considerable delegated authorities set out in its original 'lease' of the Shekou area. The China Merchants Shekou Industrial Zone Investment and Management Company was given many of the powers of a local government, including the rights to tax, approve investments, develop land and infrastructure, license imports for use in the zone, borrow abroad, issue visas and even experiment with economic reforms. The housing reforms and labour market reforms, and flexibility of controls over land use rights, were taken further in Shekou than anywhere else in China. For example, with respect to labour laws the company has labour bureau status and apart from being able to hire and fire at will, it is not bound by any of the national rules on wage scales. Any workers moving into the zone lose their standing in the national scales and have to work their way up again; elsewhere workers moving from place to place keep their place in the national scales. Pay scales in Shekou are about 30 per cent above those in Shenzhen. Evaluation methods have also been introduced which link more clearly enterprise performance and individuals' wages, bonuses and management income. Managers' contracts are voted on annually by the workers, and can in principle be cancelled by democratic vote.

Housing contracts tied to fixed-term work contracts were also first introduced in Shekou, and rents are also market-determined. The company's power over land use is sufficiently strong that it was able to block a proposal of the Shenzhen municipal government to locate a power station in Shekou. The company is the monopoly supplier of utilities in the zone, keeping the land use fees as income. It has an equity stake in many of the 380 companies in Shekou. It kept all tax revenues for the first ten years and now keeps a share of tax revenues in excess of 160 million yuan. Its reported capital rose from 60 million to 1.3 billion yuan over its first five years, all from reinvested profits. When its lease was renewed in 1990 Shekou was incorporated as a subsidiary unit of Nantou county, although it kept many of its quasi-government functions, some only on 'licence' from the Shenzhen municipal government. There are frequent disputes between the authorities of Shenzhen and those of Shekou, most recently over land use fees.

The proposals for the Yangpu Free Trade Zone in Hainan involve delegated powers similar to those obtaining in Shekou, except that the responsible agency will be a devolved branch of the provincial government. This agency will also have powers to approve investments, up to US$50 million, subject only to the need to report to the State Planning Commission, and powers to license imports and exports from the zone. It will supervise the activities of the joint-venture company, to be established by Hong Kong and Japanese property development companies, which would have the responsibility to develop the land, to attract investors to establish there and to manage the zone on a day-to-day basis.

## Experiments with markets

### Commodity markets

Commodity prices in the SEZs are mostly determined by the market. The development of commodity markets is not unique to the SEZs, but it has gone further there than in the hinterland. There are few, if any, controls on commodity prices (other than the small quantities of rationed items), or on services, in the SEZs. There has recently been an extensive development of free markets and private, collective and joint-venture shops, and tertiary sector establishments such as restaurants and hairdressers in all of the SEZs. Locally produced goods are sold free of duty and imported items are subject to only half the standard rate. Imported intermediate products and capital equipment, as already noted, are duty free to producers in the zones. In some areas, markets in producer goods have developed in which commodities are competitively priced.

Competition in most markets remains, however limited. For example, few foreign retailers have been allowed to establish in China. The first experiment with foreign retailing, other than joint-venture franchising arrangements, was approved in 1992. This is a Sino-Japanese joint venture which was given permission to open a department store in Pudong. Since then a few Hong Kong-based retailers have established outlets in Shenzhen and familiar international retailers are found, as joint ventures, in international hotels and major shopping streets. Prices of imported goods and consumer durables produced by import substitute firms in the SEZs are higher than in Hong Kong markets but lower than elsewhere in the Chinese economy. Prices of everyday consumption goods are, however, higher in the SEZs than in the rest of China, reflecting the higher incomes of workers living there.

*Factor markets*

Factor markets in the SEZs are more developed than elsewhere in China. They are still more subject to controls than market forces and still much less well developed than commodity markets. Since 1978 several experiments have, however, been introduced into the rudimentary markets for capital, labour and land. All were quickly transferred to the rest of the economy. There are currently no experiments in force in the factor markets in the SEZs which are not also operating in the hinterland, although in most cases the extent of application has gone further in the zones.

*Capital*

The capital market experiment with potentially the most far reaching effects has been the development of the joint-stock system. This was first tried in Shenzhen Special Economic Zone. State enterprises established there which satisfied strict criteria relating to capital structure, profitability and accounting practices were allowed to sell shares to the public. Outside the SEZ, firms were allowed to convert themselves into joint-stock companies but were only allowed to trade stock on a horizontal basis among similar companies. On the basis of the lessons learnt from the early development of the stock market in Shenzhen, the government of China decided to consolidate the experiment with the establishment of stock exchanges in Shenzhen and Shanghai in 1991. Initially only three stocks were approved for listing in Shanghai and seven in Shenzhen. As already noted, the experiment was further extended early in 1992 with the limited introduction of B shares on both exchanges. The adoption of regulations requiring firms wishing to be listed to subject themselves to accounting and auditing practices based on Hong Kong rules, and the requirement that firms wishing to issue B shares should be audited by foreign accounting firms, also represented a significant extension of the joint-stock experiment. The number of A and B shares traded on both exchanges, and the number of brokers accredited to each exchange are expected to increase during 1996. In July 1993 foreign brokers were introduced to the stock exchanges for the first time, as full members.

Although formal stock markets on which the general public can deal have not been approved elsewhere, informal markets have developed in many cities. In the case of Hainan the provincial government, following the advice of Deng Xiaoping to act boldly, established a stock exchange in Haikou in March 1992, with three shares being traded. Central authorities, in the person of Vice-premier Zhu Rongji, forced the closure of the exchange a few months later. Meanwhile several other cities, including Guangzhou, Tianjin, Xiamen and Beijing, are seeking approval to establish stock exchanges.

Enterprises accepted for listing are currently not allowed to sell a majority of their shares and, except for the foreign participation in joint-venture companies, boards of directors and managers continue to be official appointees with 'iron armchairs'. For the time being, the experiment is simply an additional method of raising finance for the companies and a vehicle for speculation, or simply gambling, by investors.

The significance of the reforms represented by the introduction of the joint-stock system and of stock markets and exchanges is limited. Western-style accounting and auditing practices and disclosure rules are probably the most significant reform element that have been introduced. These reforms will restrict the number of firms willing to seek listing or which could qualify for listing. To be of significance to the economic management system the experiment would have to continue to develop regulations setting out criteria for listing on the exchanges and to develop enforceable company law, with enforcement through an independent judicial system. In addition, companies and shareholders should be able to appoint directors; directors should be able to appoint and dismiss managers; and takeovers through share purchase, subject to takeover codes, should be introduced. Apart from the limited accountancy requirements for listed companies, the reforms have not so far made any significant change to the Chinese socialist characteristics of the system under which state enterprises operate.

With respect to banking, there have been very few experiments either in the zones or the hinterland in the opening up and economic reform process. As of early 1996 the banking system remained basically a centrally planned capital allocation mechanism, even though the details of its administration had changed.

The only real banking experiments have been with foreign banks. Early on, overseas banks were allowed to set up branches and representative offices, initially just in the SEZs but later also in the hinterland. The scope of their activities has been severely restricted, applying only to business in foreign currency within the regulations affecting such business. At first the banks were largely limited to arranging trade finance, but they were subsequently allowed to include raising overseas loans for import finance, within the limits set by overseas debt surveillance procedures.

Two experiments in banking are still restricted to the SEZs. The first is the existence of a joint-venture bank, the Xiamen International Bank (XIB) in Xiamen. In addition to the range of activities allowed to foreign banks, the XIB also operates in the Xiamen foreign exchange swap centre, arranges mortgages on property and, uniquely for banks with foreign funding, carries out business in local currency, albeit as yet only on an agency basis. The XIB is currently testing the limits of economic reforms by seeking a bankruptcy order in the courts against a defaulting state enterprise.

In Shenzhen, where the Hong Kong dollar operates as a parallel currency, the Hongkong and Shanghai Bank is able to operate more or less as a full service bank, including acting as a note issuer. It provides its own currency notes on demand, and via cash machines to cash card and credit card holders. This is probably the only instance anywhere in the world where a bank issues foreign currency through its cash machines; it is one development which is unlikely to spread to the hinterland.

Banks in Xiamen and Shenzhen are now providing mortgage finance although this is still limited and restricted to the residential housing market. This development is possible because a secondary market in residential property is now developing and foreclosing no longer necessarily means writing off the loans.

Despite the small amounts of capital raised through the stock market and that brought in from the hinterland by state enterprises investing in the zones, the largest share of domestic capital formation, after the use of internal funds, is financed by the banking system. Not all of this financing is allocated according to market-determined commercial principles; some is apportioned in line with plan directives and political power. Investment in fixed assets and working capital is financed by the banks even where firms have been making continuous losses and show no signs of ever recovering. This is because in the absence of an effective bankruptcy law any attempt to refuse additional credit would result in non-performing loans being turned into bad debts on the books of the banks. Profitable firms finance part of their operations with reinvested profits, but they also tend to be fully 'loaned up' and maintain the high bank debt to asset ratio now common throughout China.

*Labour*

In the case of the labour market the main experiments introduced into the zones have been the extensive replacement of lifelong tenure with short-term contracts; the ability of firms to recruit some categories of workers on a national basis and to dismiss unsatisfactory workers; in Shenzhen, the abolition of guaranteed government placement of graduates; and the development of government-run social security systems.

Experiments with labour practices have gone further in the SEZs than elsewhere in China, but the labour market is still characterized more by controls than by market forces. Of the three 'irons' that still hold sway elsewhere in the Chinese economy, the iron armchair of the cadres remains more or less undamaged. The iron rice bowl has, however, been broken for labourers. With the exception of workers in pre-existing state enterprises, mostly in Xiamen and Hainan, the majority of unskilled and semi-skilled workers in the SEZs are on two- to three-year contracts. They never obtain rights of residency. The iron pot, out of which workers take the same regardless of what they put in, is cracked but not broken. National wage scales are enforced as minima in the SEZs. Labour shortages, however, artificially engendered by restrictions on labour movement, ensure that wages, inclusive of bonuses and piece rates, are substantially higher than those paid to workers in the hinterland.

Hiring and firing practices are controlled by the labour bureaux. Firms are free to recruit skilled workers and managers from wherever they wish, although in practice the *guanxi* system applies. For unskilled and semi-skilled workers a more restrictive system applies, with tight limits being placed on employment of workers from outside the zones. In the case of Hainan the restricted market is intended to protect the interest of the island's minorities and encourage their absorption into the modern labour force. In Xiamen it is intended to protect the interests of existing workers and their children. In the greenfield SEZs, Shenzhen, Zhuhai and Shantou, the restriction is now mostly intended to prevent the zones becoming dependent on unskilled labour-intensive industries. The result is the extensive development of such industry, on a more or less unregulated, and therefore lower-cost basis, close to the zones but outside their jurisdiction.

The experiment of allowing workers more freedom of mobility between firms has been taken much further in the zones. This is partly because firms are free to dismiss workers and workers free to leave firms, either at the end of their contracts or during them with the permission of their employers (with compensation often being paid to the firm if training has been provided). Such flexibility is possible because workers' welfare benefits are not tied to an individual firm. In the first quarter of 1992, 470 of the 1,037 labour contracts signed in Xiamen were for workers changing firms, some having been dismissed and some simply seeking better jobs.

Experiments with government-run social security have been taken further in the SEZs than elsewhere in China, with the scheme, for urban workers, being most highly developed in Hainan. Most firms also run supplementary welfare, especially health, services for contract staff, who have no access to free health services provided by the local government. The ease with which firms can dismiss surplus or unsatisfactory labour is related to their classification as state enterprises or FFEs, the latter having little difficulty once they have shown good cause, whereas the former are still expected to hold on to redundant staff and even to take on workers they do not need to help keep unemployment down. The main difference for state enterprises operating in the SEZs (rather than in the hinterland) with respect to labour practices is that the greater reliance on the use of contract labour reduces the burden of having to provide the welfare services expected of state enterprises in the hinterland. Experiments with social security systems have crossed the bridge into the hinterland, but are still at a very early stage of development. For example, a social security system has been introduced into a number of state-owned enterprises in Shanghai and is now being extended to those in other parts of the country.

Workers with permanent resident rights in the SEZs prefer to be employed by state enterprises in order to gain access to the welfare benefits, whereas contract workers prefer FFEs because higher wages compensate for the more restricted welfare benefits. The gap between the average wages of state enterprises and FFEs in Xiamen early in 1992 was roughly 25 per cent, the difference between the 3,600 yuan per year paid by the state enterprises and the 4,300 by the FFEs. In addition to the wages, the FFEs also have to pay a percentage of the wage bill to the Labour Bureau to cover the government-provided social security benefits; different rates apply for wholly foreign-owned enterprises, joint ventures, and FFEs based on cooperation agreements. In Xiamen, outsiders are not allowed to work in the state enterprises. Skilled workers and graduates, on the other hand, prefer to work for FFEs as they do not need the same job security and are attracted by the higher skill premia.

Contract labour recruited from outside the zones does not enjoy all of the benefits of workers with permanent resident status. Such staff have no right to rations of subsidized food (although this is becoming less important as the range of foodstuffs subject to rationing is reduced), to housing, or to free health care provided by the local government. If they stay in a zone when a contract ends in the hope of getting a new job, they join the growing army of non-registered residents. Non-registered residents are present in large numbers in all zones.[17] They are estimated to number around half a million in Shenzhen alone, or a quarter of the total population. Those who remain in Shenzhen or Zhuhai do so illegally, as these zones are subject to border security and all residents are required to have residence permits. With no access to official or firm provided housing, non-registered residents survive in illegal sublets or, at the bottom of the market, on the streets and in shanty towns.

Many, if not most, of the contract workers are young women who work on the shift system in the labour-intensive assembly and processing factories. The gender imbalance this represents has generated some social problems, especially when the women reach marriageable age. Their productivity is alleged to decline as they fail to find partners, while they create demands for more expensive housing and social services if they do marry and have children. The Shekou Industrial Zone has an agreement with the Shenzhen municipal authority that the authority takes over the contracts of women as they reach marriageable age while Shekou recruits replacement teenagers.

The experiment of removing the placement system for university graduates is still found only in Shenzhen, where graduates have to find their own jobs, although *de facto* the practice has spread to the rest of the country. Excess demand for graduates there means that this is no real problem; most register as cadres in the hope of avoiding the vagaries of the market later in life. In other locations graduates can now opt to find their own work, bypassing the placement system, although if they do so they lose the benefits of the registration system.

*Land*

The main experiments in the land market have concerned the sale of land use rights, the development of secondary markets in land and

---

[17] They are part of the army of migrant workers moving about China in search of work. This floating labour supply is estimated at 80 million people.

property built on it, and the granting of rights to develop land commercially to foreign companies. All of these were first tried in the SEZs and all have been extended to the economy at large, although not on the same scale as in the zones.

The concept of property rights in land use was introduced in the contract responsibility system in the rural sector in the early days of opening up and economic reform. However, the sale of leases giving the right to use and develop land covering several years, initially 10 to 15 and later 30, 50 and even 70 years, including sale to foreigners, was an experiment introduced into the SEZs. The leases covered uses in the primary, secondary and tertiary sectors. Initially the prices for the leases were set by the municipal authorities, although later the more market-oriented pricing methods of auctions and tendering were introduced for some contracts. Secondary markets in the leases exist in principle, although the short time period during which they have been available means that little use has been made of these except in the residential market, particularly in Shenzhen and Xiamen. Extensive purchase of land for speculative purposes, especially in Shenzhen and Hainan by investors from Hong Kong, Taiwan and Singapore, threatens development planning and may produce a backlash in the form of regulations covering the practice of speculative investment in land use rights.

The practice of leasing land for development and commercial subletting by foreign companies was the earliest experiment with land use rights, with the granting of the ten-year lease for the development of Shekou to the China Merchants Steam Navigation Company, a Hong Kong company even if owned by the Chinese government. Resistance from conservative elements in the government prevented other such leases being granted until 1992, following the 'Spring Wind' speeches of Deng Xiaoping. A small experiment with such commercial development leases was tried in 1987 in Tianjin where part of the Economic and Technological Development Zone was leased to an American company to develop and exploit. This experiment proved unsuccessful, however, and was ended in 1992. In March 1992, the State Council finally approved the proposal to lease the Yangpu area of Hainan to a consortium of foreign firms led by two Japanese and Hong Kong firms.

Under the terms of the head lease the company would finance the development of the infrastructure and service facilities and then sell, for its own profit, the subleases for the use of the developed land, where other companies would then build factories or other commercial facilities.

The leasehold ownership of land use rights has spread beyond the SEZs, especially for FFEs, to the ETDZ and science parks in other open cities and areas. The use of auctions and tendering processes to establish the price of leases has also been extended to the hinterland, but an institutional framework for the development of a meaningful secondary market in leases and commercial buildings is not yet in place.

## Characteristics of the Chinese economy

Even though, as we have seen, the SEZs are more market-oriented than the hinterland, the markets there are still constrained and distorted.

The most constrained markets are the factor markets, where the allocation of factors of production more often reflect political priorities than market signals. Although some market elements have been introduced into factor markets, personal connections still dominate the allocation of factors of production. Labour markets are constrained by *de jure* restrictions on freedom of movement and by *de facto* restrictions caused by the absence of housing markets and centrally managed social security systems. Wages are higher in the SEZs than they would be in a market system; some firms, especially state enterprises, have excessive labour forces; and inappropriate appointments are made under the *guanxi* system. There is still no significant capital market. The stock market is likely to play only a minor role for years to come. The main source of funds is the domestic banking system which has not been effectively reformed and does not follow commercial principles. For borrowers, capital is artificially cheap; for some firms it is effectively free. In the land market, although auctions have been introduced for some land use rights, the strength of the bidders at them is partly a function of their access to artificially cheap capital from the banking or planning systems. In addition, some land use rights are allocated without charge or at discounted rates, in some cases because of the presumed existence of externalities; one example of this is the charge-free allocation of land for scientific research institutes on Caohejing ETDZ. Inadequate leasehold law also means that the 'freeholders' can and sometimes do harass lessees for surcharges to land use fees. In sum, factors are not allocated, in the SEZs as in the rest of China, in accordance with expected marginal productivity.

Commodity markets, including the markets for services, are more developed, but again there are serious impediments to their efficient operation. In the first case, access to them from the supply side is obviously affected by the distortions in the allocations of factors of production. Second, there is still substantial protection for many products and services which maintain some prices at artificially high levels. Third, the markets themselves are inefficient, partly because of the continuing presence of controls, partly because of the prohibition of foreign involvement in managing markets, and partly because the institutional frameworks for wholesale markets and markets in producer goods are still underdeveloped. Finally, some producers are simply exploiting monopoly rights granted to them by the central government, in particular import and export quotas, without which they would in many cases be unable to survive without even greater cross-subsidies or infusions of cheap or free capital.

In order to work efficiently markets need to be regulated to ensure that market exchanges take place between economic and legal equals and to prevent cheating and corruption. The legal and regulatory framework of markets in the West has developed over hundreds of years. It is also in a constant state of change as it needs to respond to changing circumstances. In China this framework is still very much in an embryonic state, as the process involves the devolution of power from the political and bureaucratic machines to the legal system. Laws to protect the interests of consumers, workers, capitalists and other economic agents hardly exist, and the development of the regulations and enforcement mechanisms needed to ensure the effective and efficient application of government policy has only just begun. The result is that even within the constraints already listed, the markets which have been developed in the SEZs, as in the rest of China, are not working as efficiently as they could.

# 4 CONCLUSIONS AND RECOMMENDATIONS

## Difficulties of evaluation

It is easy to be impressed by the physical development of the SEZs over the past 18 years (eight years in the case of Hainan), especially if one has been watching them grow throughout that period. In the three zones in Guangdong modern cities have sprung up on what had been farmland; in the case of Shenzhen a city, with adjacent areas of Bao'an county, of more than two million inhabitants, replacing the farming and fishing community of less than 60,000 that existed before the SEZ policy was announced. In Xiamen, large industrial estates have mushroomed on land hacked out of the mountainside by hand. Hainan has the feel of a dynamic modern economic frontier, and Haikou is a boom town. Seen in this light, the SEZs have indeed made great strides. In economic terms, the growth rates of gross output, exports, foreign investment, and economic and social infrastructure are the stuff that dreams are made on.

However, in assessing this performance, attention needs to be devoted to the cost of all this development, in particular the opportunity cost of the resources crammed into the SEZs. The discussion in Chapter 3 on the Chinese socialist characteristics of the zones identifies some cause for concern about the specific forms of opening up and economic reform being used to develop the SEZs. The existence of policy distortions and market imperfections suggests that some of the developments may represent a wasteful misallocation of resources. Some of the development might well have taken place in any case in response to the opening up and economic reform in general, as previously prohibited activities were allowed. The question is, how much of the development is based on comparative advantage and accurately reflects the locational advantages of the SEZs, and how much represents an inefficient use of resources, attracted by the rents created by the distortions and imperfections.

When assessing the significance of the SEZs it is also necessary to keep in mind their laboratory function. Not all experiments succeed, and the costs of any failures should be put down to the national reform process and not set directly against the internal benefits of the SEZs. On the other hand, benefits accruing in the hinterland as a result of policies successfully tested in the SEZs and transferred 'over the bridge' should also be taken into account.

There are two sources of misallocation inducing distortion. The first is the intentional distortion, that is the introduction of preferential policies intended to attract investment, but which in some cases may be redundant and result only in misallocation. The second is the interface of the two economic management systems, the socialist and the market, which generates rents that attract rent-seeking activities.

The logic behind the introduction of preferential incentive policies derives from two arguments. The first is the classic infant industry, or infant economy, argument. The second is the level playing field argument, according to which China has to offer incentives to potential investors similar to those available in countries competing for the attention of those investors. The first is used to justify tax holidays and reduced tax rates and also discounted input prices. The second is also used to justify these cost-reducing incentives, but in addition it is used to justify their continuation well beyond the time at which the steep part of the slope of the learning curve peters out. The level playing field argument is also used to justify the extension of the incentives to Chinese enterprises investing in the SEZs.

For some foreign companies the tax incentives are redundant because of double taxation agreements between their home countries and China. For others they are redundant because just as they avoid and evade taxes in their home countries, they will also seek to avoid and evade taxes in China. In addition, for many of the labour-intensive, low-skill industries which represent the majority of enterprises set up in the SEZs there are no significant learning curves; factoring set-up costs into the investment decision would have little impact. As far as Chinese enterprises are concerned the incentives are unlikely to encourage any significant increase in total investment, and will only distort the locational distribution of that investment. The opportunity cost of investing in the hinterland is artificially increased and as a result some factors of production are inefficiently moved to the SEZs, drawn by the incentives rather than by economic logic. Trickle-up rather than trickle-down is in play as capital, skilled labour and management talent move to the zones from the hinterland, attracted by the artificially high returns. Food and raw materials are also attracted into the SEZs from the hinterland, by the higher prices to be obtained there in the uncontrolled markets.[18]

The interface between the socialist and market economic management systems is also a source of resource misallocation because of the rents it generates. The socialist economic management system in China, despite the years of opening up and economic reform, is still characterized by extensive *de jure* and *de facto* controls. The dominance of controls over the movement and use of factors of production has already been noted. Rents created by the restrictions on the movement of labour and the artificially low price of capital and land attract rent-seeking activities. Those enterprises and individuals with the best connections, or *guanxi*, are the most successful at capturing these rents, as opposed to the individuals and enterprises most likely to use the resources efficiently.

Despite their privileged access to the rents which result from policy distortions, it is still estimated that more than one-third of state enterprises in the SEZs are loss-making and sustained only by access to continual injections of cheap finance by the banking system, or tax and other revenues by their government owners. Others survive, or increase their profits, by forming joint ventures with mainland Chinese compa-

---

[18] The proliferation of economic zones in 1992 and 1993 in hinterland provinces and in locations in coastal provinces without State Council approved zones was a reaction to this negative trickle-down effect. The closure of many zones in the coastal provinces constituted an attempt to cool the 'zone fever' and concentrate the positive zone effects along the Yangtse river, as part of the central government's Yangtse strategy. According to a speech by an official of the State Council Office for Special Economic Zones reported in the *South China Morning Post*, 21 August 1993, this use of economic zones was 'inspired by the success of the Special Economic Zones in the coastal regions'.

nies operating in Hong Kong, sometimes even set up by themselves in order to gain access to the privileges available to FFEs.

To these economic costs must be added the social costs of illegal activities encouraged by the freer, more flexible, environment which prevails in the SEZs. Smuggling, fraud and theft are all allegedly growth industries in the SEZs, attracted by the greater market-determined rewards and also by the wider range of goods and assets on which to spend them. The scale of corruption, on and off the zones, reached such a level that in the summer of 1993 the government of China mounted a major national anti-corruption drive which has continued into 1996.

It is difficult, if not impossible, to quantify the costs associated with SEZ development. Similarly, it is difficult to quantify the benefits to the national economy of the foreign investment which has taken place in the hinterland after having successfully tested the water in the SEZs, or the benefits from the adoption of policies on a national basis after they have been subject to successful experiment in the SEZs.[19] The actual acceptance of foreign investment was one of those experiments, but, as we have seen, there are many more: the adoption of competitive bidding for land leases and construction contracts; improved access to foreign exchange via swap markets; the development of a private housing market; moves towards a centrally organized social security system; the joint-stock company system with associated stock markets and stock exchanges; and the establishment of foreign banks. All of these policy innovations were first introduced into the SEZs and later crossed the bridge into the hinterland. The other major innovation to cross over was the zone approach itself, according to which preferential policies are restricted to specific areas, such as the ETDZs, the Science Parks, the Pudong Development Area, and the northern border towns. The 'zone within a zone' approach has also crossed over, with specialized zones being set up within the Pudong Development Area.

---

[19] The problems of obtaining zone-based data and the need to take external costs and benefits into account make it difficult to carry out standard cost benefit (CB) analysis and raise questions about the robustness of the conclusions of those CB exercises which have been carried out. Of the few examples of such work that by Shujuan Lin (1991) concluded that the Huli zone in Xiamen had a negative ratio and that by Jinghan Chen (1993) concluded that Shenzhen had a positive ratio.

## Future roles of the Special Economic Zones and policy recommendations

The Special Economic Zones have played an important role in China's opening up and economic reform process. They have been windows for the Chinese into the outside world that was for so long closed for them, and for foreigners into China – for most a totally unknown quantity. The SEZs have also been important bridges over which foreign capital, technology, goods, managers and ideas have crossed into the hinterland and over which the products of the hinterland have gained access to world markets. They have been important economic laboratories in which some of the features of Western capitalism could be tried out and, when found appropriate to Chinese conditions, allowed to cross the bridge into the hinterland. Some of the remarkable growth in China's income and trade since 1979 can be attributed to the lessons learned from looking through the window and from the results of the experiments carried out in the SEZs. Now, as pressure to create zones of various kinds mounts across the country, it is a good time to assess to roles of the SEZs and to decide what future roles they could usefully be asked to play.

The hinterland no longer needs SEZs as windows to the outside world nor does it need connecting bridges. As more of the country is opened up, as more foreign investors settle in the hinterland, as access to television expands, and as more Chinese travel abroad there is no need for special windows. And as other open cities develop connections with the outside world and build up their infrastructure, especially in Guangzhou, Shanghai and Tianjin, and as the time for Hong Kong's reintegration into China fast approaches, resources and knowledge can flow directly into and out of the hinterland without the need for special arrangements with the SEZs.

The role the SEZs must continue to play is that of economic laboratories. Experiments with market mechanisms are still at a very early stage and much remains to be done. As long as there is fear and political resistance to the introduction of market practices into China and as long as much of the hinterland remains bound up in a centrally controlled economic management system, then the SEZs will have an important role to play as locations where experiments are accepted and where conditions are more likely to ensure that these experiments can be carried out meaningfully.

The distortions highlighted in this paper are the result of incomplete experiments. Partial removal of barriers to market mechanisms may well have dramatic effects, but this does not mean that the changes are efficient, or even represent a welfare gain. The steps along the path of liberalization in the SEZs have been based on misconceptions as to the nature of markets; they have allowed remaining distortions in the system to become more profound in their impact, and have created groups with vested interests in the partially reformed system and encouraged corruption.

It is widely believed in China that creating a situation in which prices can be freely determined by the participants in the exchange process represents the introduction of Western-style markets. However, the price formation process itself is only part of the market process, and a relatively minor one on its own. Of much more importance is the  determination of access to the market and the establishment of working rules and regulations for participants in the market. All of the markets which have been created in China, even in the SEZs, have limited access and have not had rules and regulations established which are adequate to prevent the abuse of market power. The result is that the markets which exist simply create rents for those with access to them, and participants with power ensure that those rents accrue to themselves. People with good *guanxi* are able to award themselves or their connections privileged access to markets and thus ensure that the rewards of the market do not necessarily accrue to those who can make the most contribution to it. We have seen some examples of this in this paper: the distribution of trade quotas and licences, the allocation of land use rights, the granting of residency rights (with, for example, the associated privileged access to private housing markets for speculative purposes), the allocation of bank credit, and access to supplies of intermediate producer goods.

The possibility of market failure and the abuse of market power are fully appreciated in the West. Many forms of regulatory mechanisms have been devised over a long period to help overcome them. An important new role for the Special Economic Zones would be to experiment with the introduction of such checks and balances. The

System Reform Commission could be asked to develop a programme along these lines in cooperation with the zone authorities. Many experiments will need to be introduced, covering codes of practice in various markets, backed up where necessary by the force of law, which itself would involve an experimental introduction of an independent judiciary. Among the innovations needed are laws to protect consumers' and workers' rights, to require enterprises to be subjected to audit and to make full and public disclosure of their accounts and the interest of their directors, and anti-monopoly legislation and fair trading laws with associated watchdog bodies and ombudsmen. In some cases what is needed is the political will to ensure that existing laws are provided with the necessary enforcement mechanisms to ensure their effective implementation, one example being the bankruptcy laws.

One of the main problems with the development of markets in China is the lack of a cohort of Chinese citizens with knowledge of how markets operate. In particular, there is a lack of awareness of the importance of regulations. Much more attention needs to be paid to the training of market operators, perhaps in new colleges established in the SEZs. In the meantime, and while such trainees gain experience, much more reliance will have to be placed on foreign investors with the necessary experience, possibly on management contract arrangements. A major step forward would be the acceptance of more widespread foreign involvement in the commercial infrastructure of development. Experiments allowing foreign banks into the domestic currency market in the zones are believed to be at the planning stage. The scope of this experiment should be expanded to include not only foreign retailers, as has been done in some cities, but also, for example, travel agents, estate agents, labour recruitment agencies, freight and forward agencies, and insurance companies. The potential benefits from expanding competition in these markets in this way are enormous, certainly far in excess of the benefits of the existing experiments with fast food outlets − although these have established that the principle is politically acceptable. The additional benefits from the inflow of capital and know-how would be pure externalities.

Another important reform which could be introduced to improve the efficiency with which the SEZs operate would be for the government to remove as many as possible of the policy distortions for which it is currently responsible. The most important measure here would be the removal of tax and other incentives given to firms which invest in the SEZs. Firms should be encouraged to locate where it makes most economic sense and their decisions should not be distorted with tax breaks. Support for preferred locations on regional development grounds can be effected by intergovernmental transfers, such as those already in place. As a minimum, the preferential tax treatment which induces Chinese state enterprises to locate in the SEZs should be abolished. Better still would be the adoption of a standard national corporation tax for all enterprises, foreign and domestic, regardless of their location; the proposed 33 per cent rate would be sensible by international standards. Serious foreign investors will not be affected by this, because of the existence of tax-sparing arrangements in most Western countries; others who would complain because it interferes with their tax avoidance and evasion practices will find alternative remedies. The 50 per cent reduction in duties on imports sold in the SEZs, and on locally produced goods, should also be abolished. All other incentives which induce enterprises and individuals to locate in the SEZs for artificial reasons should be abolished. Only firms for which the SEZs are efficient locations would then be attracted. For these firms there is still a great deal of scope for support through the removal of obstacles to their efficient operation: freedom from production controls and reduction of bureaucratic procedures, simpler import/export procedures plus the introduction of an effective duty drawback system, and secure access to utilities and infrastructure are among the more important.

Finally, plans to increase the number of SEZs should be resisted, although the *de facto* SEZ identity of the Pudong Development Area in Shanghai should be formally recognized. The new SEZs being mooted for such places as Lhasa and Tumen should be resisted. They do not have any locational attractions for the role of economic laboratories. Similarly, proposals to develop Hainan, Shenzhen and Xiamen as freeports should be opposed, at least until these places have demonstrated that they have developed the necessary administrative and enforcement mechanisms for managing the rules and regulations needed to sustain a more efficient market-based economic management system.

# 5 ANNEX – ECONOMIC ZONES IN CHINA: A TAXONOMY

## The zones zoo

The original motive for establishing economic zones in China, in Shekou and the four pioneering Special Economic Zones, was geographically to restrict activities to which there was strong political opposition. Later, as opposition to foreign involvement in the Chinese economy became muted, the rationale of the zones came closer to that of export processing zones in other countries – the geographical restriction of economic policies more liberal than the government is prepared to see apply in the whole of the economy. The lessening of opposition to foreign involvement in the economy led to the establishment of open coastal cities, open deltas and peninsulas, and most recently open border towns and areas, including Tibet. 'Open' simply means that economic activities involving foreigners are permitted; the policy frame within which firms in open areas operate is nationally defined, available to any firm operating in such an area. In addition to the Special Economic Zones and open areas, China has established other forms of economic zone, in some cases simply to reap the benefits deriving from agglomeration economies of the industrial estate type. These offer economies of scale in terms of infrastructure or external economies with regard to common specialized services. In other cases the intention is simply to restrict the application of preferential policies. In terms of national policy, the Economic and Technological Development zones (ETDZs) and the science parks are examples of the first type, and the Free Trade Areas examples of the second. While the application of national taxation across the zones is common, by using their delegated powers the local authorities can vary the benefits of operating in the zones under their jurisdiction, for example by altering local taxes, land use charges, and charges for utilities and infrastructure. In some cases the application of national commercial policies is modified in the different types of zone. A brief guide to the different types of zone follows.[20]

*Special Economic Zones (SEZs)*

There are five SEZs: Shenzhen, Shantou and Zhuhai, all in Guangdong Province, Xiamen in Fujian Province, and Hainan, itself now a province, carved out of Guangdong in 1988. The main feature distinguishing the SEZs from the other types of zone is that they are more or less coterminous with levels of local government, municipal in the case of the first four and provincial in the case of Hainan. In addition to the local administrative authority, Hainan and Shenzhen have powers to make laws (as long as these are consistent with national laws) and all are separate planning entities – i.e., they are directly linked to the national plan and not through the provincial plan (except in Hainan, where the plans coincide). In the four municipal zones, the local government area is larger than that designated as the SEZ so that the governments have to manage SEZ and non-SEZ policies in the same jurisdiction. The SEZ areas, including all of Hainan, are separate customs areas and all movements of goods into and out of the zones are subject to licence or administrative approval, although most imports are eligible for preferential treatment. For export-oriented, 'high-tech' and foreign-funded enterprises the preferential customs and tax treatment is now identical to that which such enterprises receive elsewhere in China, except for simplified procedures and the fact that imported goods sold in the SEZs are allowed a 50 per cent reduction in tariffs, and since early 1992 imports into Shenzhen have been subjected only to *ex post* approval by customs. The two main operational features of the SEZs which distinguish them from other zones in China are the greater freedom for enterprises to manage their firms' activities and the encouragement given by the central government to the SEZ authorities to experiment with economic and social policy.

*Economic and Technological Development Zones*

The second form of economic zone to be established in China in the opening up and economic reform programmes was the Economic and

---

[20] For a detailed, although somewhat dated, account of the history of the development of the economic zone policy in China, see the State Council report (1991).

Technological Development Zone. The ETDZs were originally restricted to the 14 open coastal cities, although initially Wenzhou and Beihai were not included in the list of those permitted to establish an ETDZ. The original list, approved by the State Council in 1984 and 1985, included the three in Shanghai. Subsequently, as the opening up process spread to the inland provinces, the State Council approved the establishment of 16 more ETDZs, so that there are now 30 which have been nationally approved.[21] The most recent additions to the list include one in every provincial capital.

### High Technology Development Zones (HTDZs or science parks)

The third type of zone to be introduced was the HTDZ, or science park. By mid-1993, 50 of these had been set up with the approval of the State Council.[22] One, Caohejing New Technology Development Zone in Shanghai, is counted both as one of the HTDZs and one of the official ETDZs. The HTDZs are similar in all ways to the ETDZs except that they are usually home to government-sponsored research institutes and seek to attract high-tech industry with slightly more tax concessions than enterprises receive in the ETDZs.

### Free Trade Areas (FTAs)

Free Trade Areas are a relatively recent innovation in China. Thirteen are now thought to be operating. The first to be approved was the Waigaoqiao FTA in the Pudong Development District of Shanghai, although the Futian FTA in Shenzhen was the first to open. A second FTA in Shenzhen,

---

[21] Dalian, Qinhuangdao, Tianjin, Yantai, Qingdao, Lianyungang, Nantong, Minhang (Shanghai), Honqiao (Shanghai), Caohejing (Shanghai), Ningbo, Wenzhou, Fuzhou, Guangzhou, Zhanjiang, Kunshan, Yingkou, Weihai, Rongqiao (Fujian), Dongshan (Fujian), Shenyang, Harbin, Changchun, Wuhan, Wuhu (Anhui), Hangzhou, Chonggong (Sichuan), Xiaoshan (Zhejiang), Nansha (Gangzhou), and Dayawan (Guangdong).

[22] Beijing, Wuhan, Nanjing, Shenyang, Tianjin, Xi'an, Chengdu, Wehai, Zhingshan, Changchun, Harbin, Changsha, Fuzhou, Guangzhou, Hefei, Chongqing, Hangzhou, Gulin, Zhengzhou, Lanzhou, Shijiazhang, Jinan, Shanghai, Dalian, Shenzhen, Xiamen, Haikou, Suzhou, Wuxi, Changzhou, Foshan, Huizhou, Zhuhai, Qingdao, Weifang, Zibo, Kunming, Guiyang, Nanchang, Taiyuan, Nanning, Urumqi, Baotou, Xiangfan, Daoqing, Baoji, Jilin, Mianyang, Baoding and An'shan.

Shatoujiao, was opened in 1993. Other FTAs with State Council approval now open, or expected to be open soon, are the Jingpan FTA in Haikou, Hainan, and others in Tianjin, Xiamen, Shantou, and Dalian, the municipalities of Qingdao in Shandong Province, Zhangjiagang in Jiangsu and Ningbo in Zhejiang. The remaining two are in the cities of Fuzhou and Guangzhou. As understood in China, an FTA is a 'fenced off' zone where imports and exports can be traded freely without tariffs, duties or taxes being imposed as long as the products are not sold into the domestic market, in which case all domestic impositions are payable. Enterprises, including foreign-funded enterprises, are allowed to establish trading firms and bonded entrepôt activities as well as export-oriented production units. Beyond these basic principles the administration of the FTAs can reflect local conditions.

*State Tourist Zones*

The fourth type of economic zone officially approved by the State Council is the State Tourist Zone. Such zones receive preferential treatment to support the development of international standard tourist facilities. By the middle of 1993, 11 such zones had been approved.[23]

*Other zones*

The four types of zone listed above are the only types officially recognized by the State Council. There are also officially recognized areas within existing open locations in which special policies apply, more favourable than the policies which apply in the remaining parts of those locations. The two in question are the Pudong (also known as East Shanghai) Development District within Shanghai Open Coastal City, in which selected SEZ, HTDZ and FTA policies apply, and Yangpu within Hainan SEZ, where FTA policies and special policies towards land development by foreigners apply.

In his 'Spring Wind' speeches in South China in 1992 Deng Xiaoping referred to the failure to include Shanghai as one of the centres of open-

---

[23] Jinshitan (Dalian), Shilaoren (Qingdao), Taihu (Jiangsu), Zhinjiang (Hangzhou), Hengshadao (Fujian), Wuyshan (Fujian), Meizhoudao (Fujian), Nanhu (Guangzhou), Silver Beach (Behai), Dianchi Lake (Kunming) and Yailongwan (Hainan).

ing up to the outside world, along with the Special Economic Zones, describing it as a mistake. The mistake was partly economic in that it failed to take advantage of Shanghai's comparative advantage. In an attempt to correct it, and allow Shanghai to catch up with the south, the State Council began, in 1990, to extend preferential policies to Shanghai to encourage the opening up and reform process there. One part of the new initiative is the development of a 350 km$^2$ area of land across the Huangpu river from the old Puxi area of Shanghai, and between the Huangpu and Yangtse rivers. It is a massive development plan: the first phase alone, covering the five years from 1990 to 1995, was estimated to cost 10 billion yuan. As much of the land was farmland, the bill for turning it into an international city, complete with roads, bridges, tunnels, airport and all utilities will be enormous. It is the single most ambitious development project in China today. So far, most of the investment is being undertaken by Chinese companies and local governments, with increasing signs of large-scale involvement of foreign enterprises. Initial development in Pudong is concentrated on the three specialized zones of Waigaoqiao, Jinqiao and Lujiazui.

In the spring of 1992 the State Council approved the establishment of the Yangpu Free Trade Area in Hainan. This is a special case in that the right to exploit it has been leased to a foreign company (the only precedent for this being Shekou, but in that case the foreign company is owned by the Chinese government while in the case of Yangpu it is a Japanese/Hong Kong joint venture).

Other types of zone exist in name only. No special policies apply there. They are usually areas of existing zones, for example the Jinqiao Export Processing Zone (EPZ) in Pudong. The Shataojiao FTA in Shenzhen is also sometimes referred to as an EPZ; it is a fenced, bonded zone with a strong emphasis on foreign investment and on export orientation, and a bridge linking it directly to Hong Kong. Jinqiao, on the other hand, is an unfenced zone with individual bonded factories, and there is less emphasis both on foreign investment and on export orientation.

Pudong also has a Financial and Trade Zone, Lujiazui. This zone is intended to rebuild Shanghai's status as a regional financial and commercial centre. Wholly foreign-owned and joint-venture banks, finance companies, insurance companies and trading companies are to be established there, but as far as the State Council is concerned this would be possible anywhere in Pudong, and their concentration in Lujiazui is a decision of the Shanghai municipal government. The first foreign-funded enterprise approved in the retail trade (other than boutique shops in hotels) in China is being built in this zone. This is a joint venture between Shanghai's No. 1 Department Store and the Yaohan International Company of Japan. Directly across the Huangpu river from the Bund, the zone will have office blocks and the tallest TV tower in Asia dominating the new Shanghai skyline. Existing facilities such as the stock exchange and futures markets will move there as facilities are developed.

Confusion is caused by the imprecise terminology applied to zones, with FTAs sometimes being called bonded zones and even free ports and with local governments all over China establishing zones of their own and calling them ETDZs and HTDZs. Only those listed in this Annex had prior State Council approval. As noted in the text, the central government moved to close down many of these unofficial zones in 1993, claiming to have abolished more than 1,000 of the 1,200 which had been established along the coast. It must be assumed that those left open will receive *ex post* approval.

### The policy package

The Chinese government is in the process of moving away from a system of regional variations in economic incentives, particularly those which have favoured the coastal provinces. The move is towards sectoral incentives regardless of location. The process, however, is not yet complete.

The 1994 revisions to the foreign exchange retention system removed all geographic differentials which favoured enterprises in economic zones.

Preferential tax rates do exist in the zones, but these are generally identical in the SEZs, the ETDZs, HTDZs and Pudong. All foreign-funded enterprises outside the zones pay 33 per cent after their tax holidays expire, while in the zones all enterprises pay 15 per cent. The notional rate of 55 per cent for Chinese enterprises outside the zones is in the process of being reduced to 33 per cent. For these enterprises, the 'dividend' collected by the owners in at least some cases is adjusted so that the total 'take' remains around 55 per cent. Foreign-invested manufacturing enterprises in all zones are exempt from taxes for the first two profit-making years and pay tax at a 50 per cent reduced rate for a further three. In the SEZs only, service-sector enterprises with foreign investment are tax exempt for the first profit-making year, followed by two years at 50 per cent. And foreign banks in the SEZ and Pudong, but not the ETDZs, also have one year's exemption and two years at 50 per cent, but only if their capital exceeds $10 million. All foreign firms are exempt from profits tax on those profits which are remitted abroad. To be eligible for any of these exemptions and reductions the investment involved must be for a contracted period of at least 10 years.

Additional exemptions and/or reductions are available to foreign-funded enterprises in all zones if they introduce high-technology production processes, if they export more than 70 per cent of their production, or if they are investing in infrastructure facilities.

In addition to the exemptions and reductions of profits (or business) tax, there are also exemptions and reductions of other taxes, mainly local taxes. Apart from total exemption for foreign-funded enterprises and refunds for other enterprises of value-added tax or its equivalent, the rates of local taxes which apply vary from zone to zone, often being negotiated on an individual enterprise basis. Duty drawback is, however, payable on exports from all zones, and all zones exempt most firms from property taxes.

The tariff treatment of imports and exports varies little according to the type of zones in which a firm is located. No tariffs are charged on any item imported or exported for use in production by firms in the zones, although imports which companies sell in the SEZs for local consumption attract 50 per cent of the listed duty, and consumption goods imported by FFEs not in the SEZ attract full tariffs. Such sales are not allowed in the other types of zone. Export duties are not levied on products imported into any type of zone and then re-exported with at least 20 per cent value added by processing in the zones. Import and export procedures in the SEZs are much more simplified than they are elsewhere.

Other forms of preferential treatment which used to be restricted to the SEZs are also now available in other zones and open coastal areas. Land use rights can be assigned, sold and transferred for periods of up to 70 years in all zones. Priority access to lending from Chinese banks is also now available to all foreign-funded enterprises in all types of zone.

# REFERENCES

Chen, Jinghan (1993), 'Social Cost-Benefit Analysis of China's Shenzhen Special Economic Zone', *Development Policy Review*, Vol. 1, No. 3, pp. 261–71.

Crane, George T. (1990), *The Political Economy of China's Special Economic Zones*, Armonk NY and London: M.E. Sharpe Inc.

Khan, Zafar Shah (1991), *Patterns of Direct Foreign Investment in China*, World Bank Discussion Papers 130, Washington, DC.

Lin, Shujuan (1991), 'Application of Cost-Benefit Analysis in China: A Case Study of the Xiamen Special Economic Zone', PhD thesis, Australian National University, Canberra.

State Council Special Economic Zones Office (1991), *An Introduction to China's Coastal Open Areas*, Beijing.

Wall, David (1976), 'Export Processing Zones as a Policy Instrument', *Journal of World Trade Law*, Vol. 10, No. 5, pp. 478–89.

Warr, Peter G. (1989), 'Export Processing Zones: The Economics of Enclave Manufacturing', *World Bank Research Observer* Vol. 4, No. 1, pp. 65–88.

World Bank (1992), *Export Processing Zones*, Policy and Research Series 20, Washington, DC.

World Bank (1993), *China Foreign Trade Reform: Meeting the Challenge of the 1990s*, Report No. 11568-CHA, Washington, DC.

# PART II

## The Foreign Exchange Management System in China, 1978–95

Jiang Boke

# 6 INTRODUCTION

Soon after the Cultural Revolution, China began to focus its attention on economic growth and modernization and started an economic reform programme and open-door policy with a growth target set by the central leadership. The main thrust of China's reform programme was to use market mechanisms and foreign resources (including foreign capital and technology) to speed up the growth and modernization of the economy. In 1978 reforms were introduced first in the price system and then extended to the trade system, the agricultural sector and many other sectors of the economy. The starting point of the foreign exchange system reform was the adoption of the retention system which began in 1979, followed gradually by the introduction of more and more market components. Reform has moved from central planning domination to the use of price incentives (to encourage exports), the employment of exchange-rate alterations as a policy instrument (to encourage exports and exercise macroeconomic management), and the introduction of market mechanisms (to affect exchange rates). Fifteen years later, China's foreign exchange system has now reached an unprecedented uniformity: multiple currency practices have been cancelled, separated exchange markets have been unified, and the scope of discriminatory policies has been substantially reduced. This paper aims to give a very broad review of the reform of China's foreign exchange system. The impacts and consequences of each major reform step will be briefly analysed.

# 7 INTERNAL SETTLEMENT RATE AND DUAL RATE SYSTEM: 1981–4

On 1 January 1981, the Chinese government instituted a new exchange rate, called officially the Internal Settlement Rate (ISR), of Y2.8 to the US dollar. This was the rate offered by the Bank of China to all Chinese companies engaged in foreign trade. The ISR existed side by side with China's official foreign exchange rate, then roughly Y1.5 to the dollar, which was applied by the Bank of China to all other kinds of settlements of foreign currency transactions with the Bank of China. The Chinese government thus maintained two exchange rates, one for the settlement of the import and export trade conducted by Chinese enterprises, and the other for the settlement of all other foreign exchange transactions carried out by all Chinese and foreign companies with the Bank of China.

## The reasons for the adoption of the ISR

Why did China in effect adopt the dual-rate system – a lower rate, the ISR, for its foreign trade transactions, and a higher rate for all other foreign transactions? The first reason for introducing the ISR was to encourage exports. By lowering the exchange rate, some exports, which incurred high domestic production costs, could now be exported profitably. The second reason was to meet some requirements of China's economic reform, resulting from the decentralization of foreign trade that began in 1979. Prior to the decentralization, the Ministry of Foreign Trade (MFT)[1] was responsible for orchestrating all import and export transactions with foreign countries. This meant implicitly that all such transactions could be cleared within the MFT

---

[1] MFT, which became the Ministry of Foreign Economic Relations and Trade, MOFERT, is now the Ministry of Foreign Trade and Economic Cooperation, MOFTEC.

at any exchange rate, because the role of the exchange rate under the MFT's monopoly was only a means of account, and the MFT could subsidize exports and recoup these losses with profits earned on imports, or vice versa.

However, as the decentralization went ahead, many companies, large factories and regions were authorized to conduct foreign trade on their own behalf. It then became necessary to promulgate a new exchange rate which was uniform and suitable for all companies and regions engaged in foreign trade transactions. It was believed that a uniform exchange rate should be lower than the official rate, otherwise poor and less-developed regions and factories would suffer.

The third reason was the existence of a dual domestic price system and of a big price differential between China and the international market. Two investigations were carried out: one by the Chinese Embassy in Washington and China's central bank, the People's Bank of China (PBC) in 1980; and the other, in the same year, by a group of MOFERT economists in the ministry's Exchange Rate Policy Department.

The first investigation compared living expenses in Beijing and in Washington and reached the conclusion that 1 Chinese yuan in Beijing was equal to about US$1.25 in Washington at that time. However, MOFERT's investigation had a quite different result. For Chinese exports, US$1 was confirmed to be equal to about Y2.55, based on the records of Chinese exports in the previous five years. At that time, China's foreign trade transactions accounted for as much as 75 per cent of China's total foreign exchange transactions.[2] So MOFERT economists argued strongly for a sharp devaluation of the Chinese currency to encourage exports. Borrowing the principle suggested by James Meade in *Balance of Payments*, they argued that the number of policy targets should be the same as the number of policy instruments. Since the foreign trade transaction dominated China's total foreign exchange

---

[2] On average, during the second half of the 1970s, among China's total foreign exchange transactions, the trade account was responsible for 75 per cent, remittance from overseas Chinese for about 10 per cent, and tourism for about 5 per cent. *Source*: State Administration of Exchange Control (SAEC).

transactions, the trade account should be the only target of exchange-rate policy. It then follows that the external value of the Chinese currency should be reset according to China's trade position.

But economists from other sectors worried that a sharp currency devaluation might have a negative effect. First, a sharp devaluation would push the external value of the Chinese currency even further away from the comparison of living costs in China and abroad. Second, it might reduce the amount of foreign currency received from tourism and overseas remittances. And, third, it might harm foreign confidence in the stability of China's economy and currency.

Against this background, the State Council decided to compromise and introduce a lower internal exchange rate for the settlement of all import and export transactions conducted by Chinese enterprises with the Bank of China, while leaving the official foreign exchange rate at the previous level for all other accounts. This then is how the ISR and dual exchange-rate system came into being on 1 January 1981.[3]

*The formula of the ISR*
The ISR, after a series of careful calculations, was set at the rate of Y2.8 per dollar. The formula for its calculation is as follows:

$$ISR = \frac{(1+P)\ ER}{ED}$$

where ER is the value in terms of yuan of total exports conducted by the MFT in the previous five years (1975–9), P is the expected ratio of profits (10 per cent), and ED is the total value in terms of US dollars of the total export income in the same period.

According to this formula, the ISR was set at the rate of Y2.8 per dollar, the ISR being determined by the average cost in terms of the Chinese currency, the renminbi (RMB), in the previous five years of

---

[3] The term 'internal' means that the rate applies only to the settlement of transactions between domestic enterprises and the Bank of China, not to those involving foreign individuals or enterprises.

earning one dollar in the international market. Its advocates argued that if determined in this way, the ISR could play an active role in promoting exports. It was also believed that this formula could reflect Purchasing Power Parity (PPP), a concept which was then widely accepted in Chinese academic circles.

According to some economists, the ISR did play an active role in encouraging Chinese exports, especially those of high domestic cost, and in 1981 China's trade balance improved from a deficit of US$1.3 billion in 1980 to break even, and then turned into a surplus of US$3 billion in 1982.

## The abolition of the ISR

Since its inception in 1945, the International Monetary Fund (IMF) has played a major role in international monetary affairs. It exercises surveillance over the exchange-rate policies of member countries: according to IMF's Article IV, Section 3(b) of the Articles of Agreement and the principles and procedures set forth in IMF document 'Surveillance over Exchange Rate Policies',[4] the IMF prohibits a member from engaging in, or permitting its fiscal agencies to engage in, any discriminatory currency arrangements or multiple currency practices, except those authorized under the Articles of Agreement of the Fund and approved by the Fund in advance. Although the Articles do not clearly define the concept of a multiple currency practice, over the years detailed criteria practice as well as the Fund's policy towards their use and application have evolved from the decisions and guidelines adopted by the Executive Board, beginning with the first examination in 1947. Although the Internal Settlement Rate was only applied to the internal settlement of transactions between the Bank of China and all other domestic enterprises engaged in foreign trade, and it was not an external exchange rate according to the IMF's definition of and policy on multiple currency practices, it was still viewed as a multiple exchange-rate practice by both the IMF and international commercial

---

[4] Executive Board Decision No. 5329 (77/63), adopted 29 April 1977, in 'The Selected Decisions of the International Monetary Fund and Selected Documents, the 13th Issue', Washington DC, April 1987.

**Figure 7.1: The trend of the ISR and the OR (in terms of yuan per US dollar)**

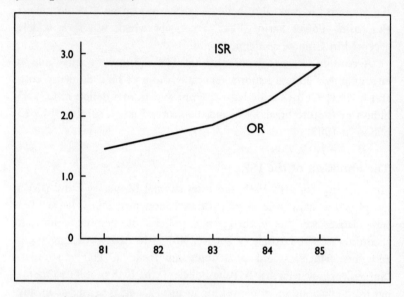

*Source*: People's Bank of China, *China Finance 1992*.

circles.[5] For instance, a Fund mission pointed out that under the terms of accession to IMF membership, China was obliged to inform the IMF of any steps it planned to take, such as this one. It claimed further that the ISR arrangement constituted a dual exchange-rate system, which required approval under IMF regulations, whereas IMF officials

---

[5] Another reason for abolishing the ISR is that the US government viewed it as a type of subsidy and strongly objected to it, claiming that it gave grounds for retaliation. In the issue of October 1983, the *Journal of International Finance* (published by the Bank of China) published an article entitled 'Foreign Responses to ISR'. This article set out a number of foreign arguments against the ISR. Foreigners firmly believed that the ISR constituted *de facto* a dual exchange-rate system. *China Business Review*, a journal of the National Committee of USA–China Relations, also published a number of articles in various issues in 1983 and 1984, arguing that the ISR was *de facto* a dual exchange rate. In my opinion, the article in *Journal of International Finance* indicated that the Chinese government was going to give up the ISR.

had only learned of this indirectly. The Fund consulted the Chinese government several times during the period 1982–4, urging it to give up the policy. In 1984, the Chinese government announced the abolition of the ISR with effect from the beginning of 1985. At that time the official exchange rate was maintained roughly at the rate of Y2.33 to US$1, and the ISR was still at the rate of Y2.8 to each US dollar. In this situation there were two choices for the government: one was to make the ISR move gradually towards the external official exchange rate (OR) and eventually equate the ISR with the OR; the other was to do the opposite – that is, move the OR towards the ISR. The government finally chose the latter. The process of exchange-rate unification is shown in Figure 7.1. It shows that during 1981–4 the ISR was persistently maintained at Y2.8, while the official external exchange rate was devalued gradually to the level of the ISR.

# 8 THE INTERMEDIATE PERIOD OF THE EXCHANGE SYSTEM: 1985–93

In 1985, China's exchange-rate system entered an intermediate period. During this period, alterations of the exchange rate were frequently employed by the central government as a policy instrument. For convenience, the following analysis is organized in two parts. The first discusses the performance and evolution of the official exchange rates, and the second deals with swap exchange rates and the foreign exchange retention system (RS). The consequences of each type of exchange reforms are analysed.

## Performance and impact: the official exchange rate

### Performance

The major characteristic of the official exchange rate during the period 1985–93 was that the rate kept going down, from Y2.8 per dollar at the beginning of 1985 to Y5.8 per dollar by the end of 1993. This downward movement can be broken down into two different stages, reflecting China's macroeconomic performance and reforms in the foreign exchange system. Stage one was from 1985 to 1990, and stage two began in 1991 and ended in 1993. In stage one, the official exchange-rate system was pegged to a basket (in which the US dollar had a dominant share) but it was adjustable. It experienced four devaluations. The idea behind it was that the external value of Chinese currency should be consistent with or based on its internal value to reflect the doctrine of PPP theory and to encourage exports. During the 1985–90 period, China's domestic inflation was high and consumer prices rose by 85.12 per cent. As domestic prices went up, the official rate was consequently devalued from Y2.8 to Y3.2 in October 1985; to Y3.7 in July 1986; to Y4.7 in December 1989; and finally to Y5.2 in November 1990. In total it was devalued by 85.71 per cent.

In stage two, the manner of the downward movement was changed from periodic and sharp adjustments to frequent and small adjustments to avoid the shocks which China had previously experienced. The rate was devalued many times, from Y5.2 to Y5.8. The total degree of devaluation was 11.54 per cent. During this time, domestic consumer prices went up by 30 per cent, leaving a gap of 18.46 per cent (30 per cent minus 11.54 per cent), which reflected the substantial reduction of the role of the official exchange rate in the settlements of foreign trade transactions (see below).

*Impact*

In China, the overall impact of the relative price changes on the trade balance induced by currency devaluation could be observed in two ways.

First, currency devaluation did not give rise to any significant reduction in the importation of foodstuffs, industrial raw materials and advanced equipment because these items are essential for people's daily life and for the chosen path of economic development. Therefore demand for them is price-inelastic. But devaluation could to some extent give rise to a reduction in those non-essential import items. The combination of the different responses of different import items to devaluation led to a relatively neutral price elasticity of overall demand for imports, leaving China's total imports little changed following each devaluation in the 1980s (see Table 8.1).

Second, on the export side, in contrast, devaluation incentives, which were stimulated by economic reform, raised the profit margins of trading companies and allowed them to buy more goods at higher prices for exporting, leading to an annual expansion of exports[6] in the 1980s, with only one minor exception in 1982 (see Table 8.1).

It should be pointed out that China's experiences with currency devaluations suggested that the trade balance was not only affected by

---

[6] It should be noted that some multilateral trade agreements may have a restrictive impact on devaluation incentives. For example, the Multi-Fibre Agreement, signed by 54 countries by the end of 1990, allows member countries to negotiate controls over textile trade in the form of quantitative quotas. In this case, devaluation may not lead to an increase in the volume of textile exports.

**Table 8.1: The evolution of China's trade balance, 1977–90 (US$ billion)**

| Year | Export | Import | Balance | Devaluation (%) |
|------|--------|--------|---------|-----------------|
| 77 | 7.6 | 7.2 | +0.4 | |
| 78 | 9.8 | 10.9 | -1.1 | |
| 79 | 13.7 | 15.7 | -2.0 | |
| 80 | 18.3 | 19.6 | -1.3 | |
| 81 | 22.0 | 22.0 | 0 | 80 |
| 82 | 22.3 | 19.3 | +3.0 | |
| 83 | 22.2 | 21.4 | +0.8 | |
| 84 | 26.1 | 27.4 | -1.3 | |
| 85 | 27.4 | 42.3 | -14.9 | 14 |
| 86 | 30.9 | 42.9 | -12.0 | 16 |
| 87 | 39.5 | 43.2 | -3.7 | |
| 88 | 47.5 | 55.2 | -7.7 | |
| 89 | 52.5 | 59.1 | -6.6 | 27 |
| 90 | 62.1 | 53.4 | +8.7 | 11 |

*Source*: For 1977–86 data, *Statistical Yearbook of China*, 1987, p. 591; for 1987–90 data, IMF, International Financial Statistics (IFS), 1994, pp. 64–5.

the relative price changes induced by currency devaluations, but was also substantially affected by other macroeconomic policies such as expenditure policy. The appropriate mix of expenditure reduction and expenditure switching policies is the key for devaluation to be successful, both in terms of improving the trade balance and fostering economic growth. This proposition is supported both by the general trend of imports and exports, which followed the 'up and down' cycle of the national economy in the 1980s in general, and by several individual cases. For instance, in 1981 and 1989, facing ever-increasing inflationary pressure and continuous trade deficits, the Chinese government substantially cut its expenditures to control excess demand while simultaneously devaluing its currency in order to stimulate export production. With such an appropriate policy mix, and a one-year time lag, China's imports were subsequently reduced while exports still experienced an increase.

From the above analysis it seems safe to draw two conclusions. First, China's experiences with currency devaluations in the 1980s provided no evidence that devaluation would exert an adverse impact on the trade balance. On the contrary, devaluations contributed to the expansion of exports, and hence to national economic growth. Second, the proper mix of different types of policy instruments is a precondition for devaluation to work effectively.

## Performance and impact: the retention system and swap exchange rates

### Retention system

Before 1979, the basic feature of China's foreign exchange system was the state monopoly. That is to say, the Chinese central government had complete control over all income and expenditure of foreign exchange throughout the country. Under the state monopoly, all foreign exchange income of any enterprise had to be submitted to the state (via the Bank of China), and then the state allocated foreign exchange according to its plan. This old system was not compatible with the market-oriented economic reform which started in 1978. In addition, this system did not encourage enterprises to work harder to earn more foreign exchange. It was believed that this system would hinder the implementation of China's open-door policy. For these reasons, as a substitute for the state monopoly system, the retention system (RS) was adopted in 1979.

The retention system is complicated. According to this system, if an enterprise is successful in exporting its products and hence obtaining a certain amount of foreign exchange, it will be permitted to retain for its own disposal some percentage of the total amount of such foreign exchange earnings. For example, if an exporter earned $1 million from international markets, under the retention system it would be permitted to retain, say, 30 per cent for its own disposal, while the residue, 70 per cent, would still be submitted to the government.

How much an exporter could actually retain from its total foreign exchange income depend on the retention percentage system. Different regions, industrial sectors, and factories were entitled to different retention percentages. Normally, the five special economic zones, poorer and remote regions such as Tibet and Xingjiang, and new, advanced and high-tech products were entitled to higher percentages. In short, the percentage was determined on a case-by-case basis, and was not nationally uniform.

It can be imagined that by comparison with the system prior to 1979, the retention system played a more active role in encouraging exporters because it permitted them to keep a certain portion of their foreign exchange income, thus enabling them to enjoy more freedom to import what they wanted from the international markets.

However, a single exporter might be unable to hold and keep its retained foreign currency if it did not need to import goods to continue its production, or if the amount of retained foreign currency was not exactly equal to the amount it wanted at any given time. This gave rise to the necessity of foreign currency swaps between (tentative) surplus and (tentative) demands. The swap business thus became necessary for the RS to work in practice.

*Swap exchange rates*

The swap business started in October 1980. Owing to the absence of any established swap centres at that time, business was conducted through the Foreign Exchange Service Department of the Bank of China. Soon after the retention system was adopted, the Bank of China and SAEC jointly promulgated the Provisional Foreign Exchange Regulations in 1981. The main points are:

(a) Swap business is permitted and encouraged, but it must go through the Bank of China.
(b) Only state-run enterprises are allowed to conduct swap transactions.
(c) Only retained foreign exchanges are allowed to be sold to the Bank of China for swap purposes.
(d) The fluctuations of swap prices can be no more than 5 per cent above the Internal Settlement Rate (Y2.66 per dollar) or 10 per cent below the ISR (Y3.08). Within the scope of this limit, prices may be negotiated between buyers and sellers.

Since the promulgation of the regulations, the swap business experienced four episodes: (1) start (1981–2); (2) growth (1983); (3) decline

(1984); and (4) stagnation or suspension (1985). The major reason why the swap business declined was the tight control over the swap prices: Y3.08 per dollar was too low to attract sellers of foreign exchange. So in 1986, the scope of price fluctuations was extended to Y1 per dollar above or below the official exchange rate. For example, if the official exchange rate was Y3.7 per dollar, then the scope was from Y2.7 to Y4.7 per dollar. In 1988, the limit of the scope was further extended to Y2 above or below the official exchange rate, and soon fully lifted by the 'Regulations Concerning Foreign Exchange Swaps', which were adopted from 9 March 1988.

The major modifications of the 1988 Regulations, compared with the 1981 Regulations, are as follows:

(a) Swap transactions are conducted at swap centres (if available) instead of going through the Bank of China.
(b) Swap rates are principally determined by the market forces.
(c) The PBC may intervene in swap rates by selling or buying foreign exchanges at swap centres through a newly established foreign exchange balance account.
(d) A series of subsequent documents soon reduced the restriction on access to the swap market. The scope of permitted transactors was expanded from a few pre-approved enterprises to almost every foreign and domestic enterprise and official agent. From 1991, even private individuals were allowed to enter the swap market.

In addition to the regulation changes, swap centres began to appear. The first centre was set up in Shenzhen on an experimental basis in November 1985. Subsequently, they were set up in Shanghai (November 1986) and Beijing (April 1988). The number of swap centres grew very rapidly so that, by the end of 1989, about 90 of them had been established throughout China.

For the reasons stated above, the swap transactions began to boom. Swap exchange rates had been covering more and more foreign exchange transactions. For instance, the total amount of foreign exchange swap in 1987 across the country reached US$4.2 billion, within which foreign enterprises swapped US$330 million. In 1988,

**Table 8.2: Expansion of the swap market (US$ billion)**

|  | 1987 | 1988 | 1989 | 1990 | 1991 | 1992 |
|---|---|---|---|---|---|---|
| Total value of swap amount | 4.2 | 6.3 | 8.6 | 13.1 | 20.4 | 25.0 |
| Increase (%) | — | 50.0 | 36.5 | 52.3 | 55.7 | 22.8 |
| Total value of China's trade[a] | 82.7 | 102.7 | 111.6 | 115.5 | 133.1 | 165.5 |
| Shares of swap in total trade (%) | 5.1 | 6.1 | 7.7 | 11.3 | 15.3 | 15.1 |

[a] Includes imports and exports.
*Source*: Swap data from SAEC, trade data from IFS 1994.

the total amount of foreign exchange swap increased further, to US$6.28 billion, within which foreign enterprises swapped US$882 million. In 1989, the total amount of swapped foreign exchange increased again to US$8.566 billion, within which foreign-funded enterprises swapped US$1,570 million. In 1990, the total swapped foreign exchange rose to US$13.1 billion, a 50 per cent increase. As a result, the share of the swapped foreign exchange in China's total trade (imports and exports) increased from 5.1 per cent in 1987 to over 15 per cent in both 1991 and 1992.

Obviously, since the introduction of the swap rate, China had turned back again to a new kind of dual exchange-rate system. In this system, one rate was fully adjusted by the monetary authority and the other was mainly determined by market forces. Owing to the many different retention percentages in existence, China's foreign exchange system was in fact not a dual one, but a multiple one. The actual exchange rates were as calculated in Box 8.1.

Under this retention percentage system, by selling foreign exchange on the swap market, some exporters got more domestic currency while some got less. Thus, this system played a role in encouraging certain sectors of industry. From 1987 to 1991, China's total exports increased by 82.2 per cent. The export of products with a lower retention per-centage (primary goods) increased by only 22.2 per cent, while the

## Box 8.1: China's foreign exchange-rate system

**In 1989, the retention percentages by locality:**      **Actual Exchange Rates (AER)**

- 100% for Tibet;      AER=1xSR[a]
- 80% for Special Economic and Technological Development Zones;      AER=0.8xSR+0.2xOR[b]
- 50% for minority populated regions such as Inner Mongolia, Xinjiang, Guangxi, Ningxia, Qinghai, Guizhou, and Yunnan;      AER=0.5xSR+0.5xOR
- 30% for provinces with special policy status, including Guangdong and Fujian;      AER=0.3xSR+0.7xOR
- 25% for rest of the country;      AER=0.25xSR+0.75xOR

**In 1989, the retention percentages by industrial sectors:**      **Actual Exchange Rates (AER)**

- 100% for selected electronic groups, defence, science, and educational sectors, & foreign contract projects;      AER=1xSR
- 100% for machine-building and electronic sectors undertaking reform programmes as well as all foreign investment firms;      AER=1xSR
- 90% for ship production sector;      AER=0.9xSR+0.1xOR
- 80% for light industry, arts, crafts, and garment sectors;      AER=0.8xSR+0.2xOR
- 65% before and 100% after meeting the export target for machine-building and electronic sectors;      AER=0.65xSR+0.35xOR
- 30% for tourism-related sector;      AER=0.3xSR+0.7xOR
- 25% for all others.      AER=0.25xSR+0.75xOR

[a] SR = swap rate.
[b] OR = official rate.
*Source*: Jiang Boke, *International Finance* (Shanghai: Fudan University Press, 1994) p. 104.

**Table 8.3: Rate of export increase, 1987–91 (%)**

| | |
|---|---:|
| All exports | 82.2 |
| Primary goods (lower retention percentage) | 22.2 |
| Manufactured goods (higher retention percentage) | 112.4 |
| **Group 1 (retention percentage: 80%)** | 115.5 |
| Garments | 134.3 |
| Cotton products | 65.8 |
| Toys | 113.1 |
| Sport products | 241.0 |
| Leather shoes | 422.5 |
| **Group 2 (retention percentage: 100%)** | 237.5 |
| Family electronic goods | 211.3 |
| Communication products | 586.9 |
| TV sets | 118.7 |
| **Group 3 (retention percentage: 100%)** | 235.1 |
| Sets of machine equipment | 240.8 |
| Ships and related parts | 102.8 |
| Vehicles and related parts | 519.1 |
| Electric generators | 641.9 |
| Lifter machines | 488.5 |

*Source*: MOFERT, *International Trade Statistics*, 1990, pp. 394–5; MOFERT, *China Foreign Economic and Trade Statistical Year Book* 1992, pp. 405–11.

export of products with a higher retention percentage (manufactured goods) increased by 112.4 per cent. Furthermore, among the manufactured exports, the export of machine-building and electronic goods increased more than that of the light industry, arts, crafts and garment sectors. Owing to the absence of systematic statistics, the fastest increasing exports are selected here to illustrate the impact of the exchange system on China's industry (see Table 8.3).

Table 8.3 shows that the swap rate and retention system was most advantageous to the machine and electronic industry sectors. Its effectiveness was just like a currency devaluation. But this system is discriminatory, and forced exporters to compete with one another on an unequal basis. One repercussion of such a discriminatory system must be serious distortions in relative prices which, in turn, would affect the economic efficiency of resource allocations and productivity growth.

This system was in effect a selective fiscal/subsidy proxy for a uniform devaluation. Its adverse consequences would inevitably cause problems and hence constrain the long-term management of the system itself.

In theory, devaluation is assumed to play a role in improving the trade balance through the price adjustment mechanism, which analyses the process in terms of the elasticities approach. Within this partial equilibrium framework, it is easy to see that devaluation is exactly equal to a uniform *ad valorem* subsidy to all exports and simultaneously a uniform *ad valorem* tax on all imports. In this regard, there is no difference between a currency devaluation and a uniform fiscal/subsidy proxy for devaluation in the effect on the trade balance, but the administrative cost is likely to be higher for the latter. However, there is one significant difference between the two measures: when the elasticities are high, a devaluation is obviously superior to a discriminatory subsidy policy, because in this case a devaluation is at once an efficient instrument both for raising output and for altering the structure of production; when the elasticities are low, on the other hand, a selective or discriminatory fiscal/subsidy proxy might be superior to a devaluation. But the problem is that, as we will see below, a tax/subsidy measure is likely to be misused because in practice, especially in an economy where prices are distorted, it is very difficult to sort out those which are export products that should be subsidized and those which are import products that should be taxed. Such misuse, together with the higher administrative cost brought about by a discriminatory proxy, may more than offset any advantages of a discriminatory policy, especially when elasticities are not low.

Lower effectiveness and adverse consequences of discriminatory fiscal subsidies on resource allocation and productivity growth, compared with a straightforward devaluation, can also result from other causes:

(1) The retention percentage for an enterprise or availability of foreign exchange at a cheaper official exchange rate for an importer may sometimes be misdirected. Lobby skills and individual officials' knowledge of the importance of relevant products or import items can also influence the retention rate. This is quite likely to lead, to a greater or lesser extent, to an inappropriate use of discriminatory policy. In addition, the complicated administrative procedure would create much bureaucratic work. A lot of contradictory documenta-

tion would often confuse the implementation of the discriminatory policy.

(2) The swap exchange-rate system, combined with a retention percentage system, is likely to play some role in encouraging inefficient enterprises. The level of technology of enterprises in remote areas is much lower than those in the coastal area. But remote enterprises are entitled to a much higher retention percentage, resulting in inefficient resource allocation and lower productivity in aggregate.

(3) In China, most exporters, as reflected in the composition of China's exports, are involved in the textile, food-processing, light industrial, handicraft, and low-tech machine sectors, whereas many major importers come from high-tech, infrastructural, and heavy industrial sectors. The swap exchange rate has turned out to favour exporters, hence is unfavourable to high-tech, infrastructural and heavy industrial sectors; this, in turn, is unfavourable to China's long-term economic development.

Obviously, the fundamental causes of China's foreign exchange shortage cannot be removed by the discriminatory system. From 1988 the swap rate and official rate began to diverge. Under the pressure of fast economic growth, the gap between the two was widening considerably, and fluctuations of swap rates were sometimes very sharp, constituting a threat to macroeconomic stability. In 1993, China's foreign exchange system was faced with a number of threats. First, the volume of retained foreign exchange substantially exceeded the foreign exchange reserve. The retention system was criticized by both business and academic circles. A national appeal emerged for the replacement of the quota retention system (QRS) by the cash retention system (CRS).[7] However, if the CRS were implemented the foreign exchange reserve would be exhausted.

---

[7] The quota retention system is one in which foreign exchange income is retained in the form of a certificate, not in the form of foreign currency itself. That is to say, the retained foreign exchange must be sold to the government in exchange for domestic currency and a retention certificate. When the exporter wants to use his retained foreign exchanges, he can purchase them back with the certificate and domestic currency. The cash retention system, in contrast, is the system in which an exporter can retain his foreign exchange income in the form of foreign currency itself.

**Figure 8.1: Divergence of dual rates and fluctuations of swap rate in 1993**

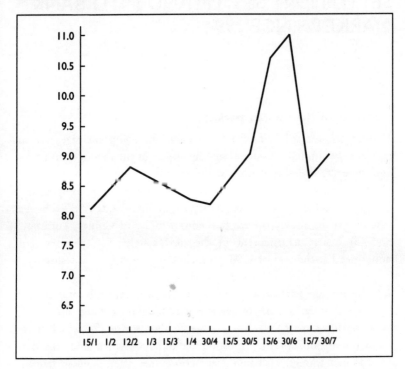

*Source*: SAEC.

Second, the swap rates fluctuated sharply in the first half of 1993, causing foreign exchange markets to become quite unstable. At the beginning of the year, the gap between the official rate and swap rate was about Y1, but on 19 June it jumped to Y5.2 (see Figure 8.1).

Third, the official exchange rate was under heavy pressure to devalue owing to high domestic inflation and lower swap and parallel rates. On 20 June, the SAEC was forced for the first time to intervene in the swap market: it sold $70 million in the morning, and a further $75 million in the afternoon. This was a signal that the government was determined to take actions to keep the market stable. The outcome was positive: the level of the swap rate fell next day to Y8.7, where it remained for the second half of the year.

# 9 THE FOREIGN EXCHANGE SETTLEMENT SYSTEM AND INTERBANK MARKET SINCE 1994

## Contents of the reform package

During the second half of 1993 a new and comprehensive reform package was under consideration. The targets of the new reform package were (1) the elimination of the *de facto* multiple exchange rates; (2) the creation of a more equitable environment for competition; (3) the introduction of more market components into the exchange system; (4) the move towards free convertibility of Chinese currency; and (5) easier management of the new system. The package was announced at the end of 1993. Its main components are as follows:

(a) The foreign exchange retention system is completely replaced by the settlement system, under which all foreign exchange income of enterprises apart from foreign invested enterprises, for which there is a transitional period,[8] must be sold to banks which are licensed to conduct foreign exchange transactions (hereafter, licensed banks). When an enterprise needs foreign exchange to conduct transactions under the current account, it can freely purchase it with domestic currency and a submission of the relevant and effective documents or certificates (for example, import contracts) from licensed banks. The PBC set each licensed bank, in turn, an upper limit for its foreign currency holdings which cannot be extended.

(b) The swap market is replaced by the interbank foreign exchange market on which licensed banks buy or sell their foreign currencies with one another or with the PBC to manage their foreign currency liquidity positions and to meet the top limit requirement of the PBC.

---

[8] The transition period was originally one year, but it has been extended, for reasons explained in the text.

The foreign exchange rate is determined by demand–supply interactions on the market. The national centre of the interbank exchange market, the China Foreign Exchange Trade Centre, was set up in Shanghai and is connected with over thirty cities across the country.

(c) The central bank, the People's Bank of China, has set up the Open Market Operation Desk (OMOD) for transactions on the interbank market. The functions of the OMOD are twofold. First, it manages banks' foreign currency liquidity position by acting as the last-resort buyer and supplier; and, second, it monitors and intervenes to manage the interbank exchange rate to keep the market and macroeconomy stable. In 1994, the OMOD intervened in the market very frequently.

### Consequences

This reform package and its subsequent implementation have been viewed by some Western economists as a great success in China's transformation to a market economy because it has abolished the multiple currency practice and signals that China's monetary authority has put more reliance on the use of market mechanisms to convey its monetary policy. But within China, this reform package has triggered a great deal of dispute as to its effectiveness. Its advocates think that this package has created a fairer basis for competition among enterprises, that it is helpful in removing price distortions, and that it can also contribute to RMB convertibility which, in turn, can support further reform and the opening up of China's economy. The opposite view, however, is that it is important for financial reform to take an appropriate place in the progress of transformation and liberalization of the whole economy.[9] In

---

[9] From the beginning of 1994, the Chinese government simultaneously adopted five reform packages in the following areas: fiscal, social security, financial, foreign trade, and the state-owned (real) asset management system, against the background of high inflation and macroeconomic instability. This led to discussions on the optimal order of economic liberalization. See Jiang Boke, 'The Order of Liberalizations and RMB Convertibility in Economic Research', CASS, Beijing, March, 1994, pp. 20–38; and 'Procedure of Foreign Exchange Management System Reform', in *People's Daily Internal Reference*, Beijing, February, 1994, pp. 1–12.

**Figure 9.1: Mundell-Fleming model**

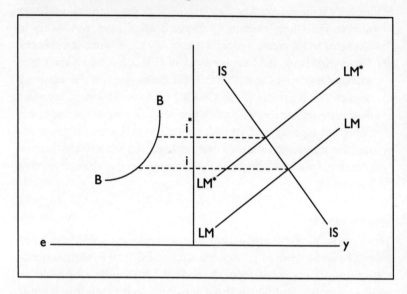

particular, it is argued that the reform of the enterprise ownership system and the establishment of a sound fiscal control system should take priority over financial reform, and that the speed of the 1994 reforms was so fast that it has caused severe instability. The domestic inflation rate in 1994 reached 24 per cent, much higher than the 1993 rate (18 per cent), and the 1994 target rate set in 1993 (15 per cent).

Personally, I support the reform package in principle but consider that its method of implementation is inappropriate. The main points that should be noted are: (1) the settlement system was implemented too fast, which has led directly to inflationary pressure; (2) the interbank exchange rate was kept so rigid that its role as a policy instrument was lost; (3) the implementation of the reform package should be accompanied and supported by some other kinds of policies, especially a fiscal policy. In a fixed or a *de facto* fixed exchange-rate system, as shown in the Mundell-Fleming model analyses (see Figure 9.1), the curve BB is a line indicating the combinations of domestic interest rate *i* and exchange rate *e*, which lead to equilibrium in the balance of payments. In this situation, monetary policy itself is ineffective in reducing inflationary pressure. If the capital market is integrated, the monetary tightening induces a leftward shift of the LM schedule. Consequently, the domestic interest rate rises from $i$ to $i^*$ while exchange rate $e$ is maintained unchanged, which induces capital inflows.[10] Through the settlement system, the money supply increases and the LM schedule moves back from LM$^*$ to LM. Since the middle of 1993, the PBC has been implementing a tight monetary policy, but its anti-inflationary effect was completely offset by the method of implementation of the reform package. This can be illustrated by the diagram in Figure 9.1.

First, from the beginning of 1994, the interbank exchange rate has been maintained at the level of Y8.55 by the OMOD's strong interventions. In 1994, the share of the OMOD's transactions in the interbank market amounted to nearly 70 per cent with the result that the fluctuations of the interbank exchange rate have never exceeded 2 per cent. China has been running a *de facto* fixed exchange-rate system. As analysed above, in a open economy, when the exchange rate is fixed and the interest rate rises, capital inflows are induced. These will be amplified if the economy grows fast and demand is strong. This was the case in China. In 1994, contract capital inflows reached over Y900 billion while actual inflows reached Y300 billion – in both cases a 50 per cent increase on the previous year. According to the new regulations set forth in the reform package, the inflow of capital of non-foreign-invested enterprises in the form of funds (not capital goods or equipment) had to be switched immediately into Chinese currency through licensed banks. Licensed banks had to resell their foreign currencies to the central bank, and the central bank, in turn, had to sell domestic currency. This formed a source of additional money supply. Furthermore, the reform package cancelled the foreign currency accounts of all non-foreign-invested enterprises and government agents and all their foreign currency deposits were required to be con-

---

[10] The Mundell-Fleming model provides a detailed analysis of the role played by international capital mobility in determining the effectiveness of fiscal and monetary policies under alternative exchange-rate regimes. For an exposition and evaluation, see Frenkel and Razin (1987).

verted into domestic currency in a short transitional period (before the end of August 1994). This constituted another source of foreign exchange supply in the interbank market and led to a further increase in the money supply.

In 1994 the OMOD, constrained by the settlement system, bought in a total of US$30 billion and sold out Y256.5 billion (the average exchange rate was Y8.55). In this way the stock of high-powered money increased by Y256.5 billion and the supply of broad money (M2) increased by Y770 billion, if one assumes that the monetary multiplier is three.

Second, the swap rate and official rate were unified too quickly and the interbank rate was maintained at too low a level (Y8.7/$1), causing a sharp devaluation in a short period. In 1993, the average annual swap rate was at the level of Y8.7 and covered about 60 per cent of China's total import settlements, while the average official rate was maintained at the level of Y5.7 and covered about 40 per cent of China's total import settlements. The average annual rate for all import settlements in 1993 can be calculated as follows:

1993 Average Annual Rate = Y8.7 x 60% + Y5.7 x 40% = Y7.5

That is to say, the RMB exchange rate was devalued by 16 per cent in 1994, from Y7.5 to Y8.7. Furthermore, by extending the analytical period, we find that the Chinese currency was devalued by 46.6 per cent within only two years (1992–4) (see Table 9.1). The sharp devaluation reinforced the inflationary pressure and constituted another major source of domestic inflation in 1994.

Owing to high domestic inflation, the implementation of the reform package has been slowed. Evidence of this is that the transitional period for transferring foreign-invested enterprises into the settlement system has been extended from the original date of the beginning of 1995. The fear that foreign-invested enterprises hold large quantities of foreign currency and that the switch would force the central bank to buy this in, selling out domestic currency, thereby probably leading to loss of control of the supply of base money, has forced the SAEC to suspend the application of the settlement system to foreign-invested

## Table 9.1: Actual devaluation magnitude: 1992–4

1994 interbank rate (beginning of the year) = Y8.7
1993 average annual rate = Y8.7 x 60% + Y5.7 x 40% = Y7.5
1992 average annual rate = Y6.3 x 55% + Y5.5 x 45% = Y5.94

| Devaluation magnitude | Inflation rate (%) |
|---|---|
| From 1992 to 1993, RMB was devalued by 29.6% | 6.0 |
| From 1993 to 1994, RMB was devalued by 16.0% | 18.0 |
| From 1992 to 1994, RMB was devalued by 46.5% | 24.8 |

*Source*: SAEC and author's estimate.

enterprises. Moreover, the settlement system itself is now under modification. The top limit of each bank's foreign currency holdings looks likely to be raised. If implemented, this change could help mitigate the pressure on base money increases.

# 10 CONCLUSION

In the past fifteen years, China's foreign exchange system has experienced three phases: (1) the dual exchange-rate system under which the ISR and official rate coexisted; (2) the intermediate period in which the alterations of exchange rate were frequently employed as a policy instrument, and the retention system and the market-determined swap rate played more and more important roles in foreign exchange allocations and settlements of foreign exchange transactions; and (3) the foreign exchange settlement system and interbank exchange-rate system in which discriminatory policies have been reduced substantially and the exchange rate is determined in the interbank exchange market; open market operations of the central bank have also started. Of course, each phase always caused new problems, but the system itself is now moving steadily towards a market orientation.

The changes were driven by two factors: one from China's domestic sector and the other from the external sector. In the domestic field, there were comprehensive economic reforms; thus the foreign exchange management system itself also had to change to fit in with the whole reform programme. As to the external field, China was becoming more and more open, and the influence of the international community had become an important contributory factor in the changes to China's foreign exchange management system. This was reflected not only in the unification of dual exchange rates in 1984, as stated above, but also in the subsequent changes of the system. For example, the swap rate actually constituted a dual-rate system but, encouraged by the IMF, China used it as a transitional phase. As an IMF official pointed out:

> Although the Fund principally opposes the multiple exchange rate practices, the introduction of the swap exchange market is viewed as a way for

a centrally planned economy to move towards the market economy. The Fund would not oppose such a transitional process, but would hope that it could be completed in a due time.[11]

Another example is the movement towards the convertibility of the RMB. This requirement is listed in Article VIII of the Articles of the Agreements of the Fund, and it is also reflected in the documents of the GATT (now World Trade Organization). Since China wishes to gain WTO membership and to expand its foreign economic relations, it has promised that currency convertibility will be realized under the current account by the year 2000.

In short, China's foreign exchange management system will continue to become more market-oriented through the requirements of continuous economic reform and the economic interdependence of its economy. To ensure that such a move is smoothly conducted and realized, the support of reforms in all other sectors, particularly through the understanding of the international community, and the creation of more policy instruments with market characteristics, are necessary. In the future, these are likely to become burning issues for economic research.

---

[11] Interview with Dr Hoe Ee Khor, IMF senior economist in the Asia Department, China Division, Washington DC, 17 October 1990. Another senior IMF official, Mr Zhang Zixiang, the executive director for China, expressed a similar opinion during the interview.

# REFERENCES

Bhagwati, Jagdish N. (1978), 'Foreign Trade Regimes and Economic Development: Anatomy and Consequences of Exchange Control Regimes', New York: National Bureau of Economic Research.

Byrd, William (1987), 'The Impact of the Two-Tier Plan/Market System on Chinese Industry', in *Journal of Comparative Economics*, September, pp. 295–308.

Cooper, R. N. (1971a), 'Currency Devaluations in Developing Countries', Princeton Essays in International Finance, No. 86.

Cooper, R. N. (1971b), 'Devaluation and Aggregate Demand in Aid-Receiving Countries', in J. N. Bhagwati, R. W. Jones, R. A. Mundell, and J. Vanek, eds, *Trade, Balance of Payments, and Growth: Papers in International Economics in Honor of Charles P. Kindleberger*, North-Holland, pp. 355–76.

Cooper, R. N. (1973a), 'An Assessment of Currency Devaluation in Developing Countries', in Gustav Ranis, ed., *Government and Economic Development*, Yale University Press, pp. 472–512.

Cooper, R. N. (1973b), 'An Analysis of Currency Devaluation in Developing Countries', in Michael B. Connolly and Alexander K. Swoboda, eds, *International Trade and Money*, University of Toronto Press, pp. 167–96.

Desai, Padma and Jagdish Bhagwati (1981), 'Three Alternative Concepts of Foreign Exchange Difficulties in Centrally Planned Economies', in Jagdish N. Bhagwati, ed, *International Trade: Selected Readings*, Cambridge, MA: MIT Press.

Edwards, Sebastian (1984), 'The Order of Liberalization of the External Sector in Developing Countries', in *Essays in International Finance*, No. 156 (Princeton).

Fleming, J. Marcus (1971), 'Dual Exchange Rates for Current and Capital Transactions: A Theoretical Examination', in his *Essays in International Economics* (Cambridge, MA: Harvard University Press), pp. 296-325.

Fleming, J. Marcus (1974), 'Dual Exchange Markets and Other Remedies for Disruptive Capital Flows', in *IMF Staff Papers*, Vol. 21, No. 1, March, (Washington, DC: International Monetary Fund), pp. 1-27.

Frenkel, Jacob A. and Assaf Razin (1985), 'Aspects of Dual Exchange Regimes', Institute for International Economic Studies (Stockholm: University of Stockholm) seminar paper No. 335.

Frenkel, Jacob A. and Assaf Razin (1986), 'The Limited Viability of Dual Exchange Rate Regimes', NBER working paper No. 1902 (Cambridge, MA: National Bureau of Eononomic Research).

Frenkel, Jacob A. and Assaf Razin (1987), 'The Mundell-Fleming Model: A Quarter Century Later', in *IMF Staff Papers*, Vol. 34, No. 4, December (Washington, DC: International Monetary Fund), pp. 567-620.

Gros, Daniel (1988), 'Dual Exchange Rates in the Presence of Incomplete Market Separation: Long-Run Effectiveness & Policy Implications', in *IMF Staff Papers*, Vol. 35, No. 3, September (Washington, DC: International Monetary Fund), pp. 437-60.

Jiang Boke (1994), *Studies in RMB Convertibility* (Shanghai: Lixing Press).

Jiang Boke (1995), *China Money Market* (Shanghai: Fudan Development Institute).

Johnson, O. E. G. (1976), 'The Exchange Rate as an Instrument of Policy in a Developing Country', in *IMF Staff Papers*, Vol. 23, No. 2, July, Washington, DC: International Monetary Fund, pp. 334–48.

Kiguel, Miguel A. and J. S. Lizondo (1986), 'Theoretical and Policy Aspects of Dual Exchange Rate System', *World Bank Discussion Paper*, Report No. DRD201, Washington, DC: World Bank.

Laker, John F. (1981), 'Fiscal Proxies for Devaluation: A General Review', in *IMF Staff Papers*, Vol. 28, No. 1, March (Washington DC: International Monetary Fund).

Lanyi, Anthony (1975), 'Separate Exchange Markets', in *IMF Staff Papers*, Vol. 22, No. 3, November (Washington, DC: International Monetary Fund), pp. 714–49.

McKinnon, Ronald (1991), *The Order of Economic Liberalization: Financial Control in the Transition to a Market Economy* (Baltimore: Johns Hopkins University Press).

Wilson, J. S. G. (1993), *Studies in Money Markets* (London and New York: Routledge).

Zhou Zhengqing (1992), *Studies on China Monetary Policy* (Beijing: China Financial Press).

# PART III

## China's Trade Policy Reforms and their Impact on Industry

Yin Xiangshuo

# 11 INTRODUCTION

China's foreign trade has developed rapidly since the implementation of reform and opening-up policies in 1978.[1] Until then, the focus of general economic policy was rapid industrialization through self-reliance. As a part of the general economic development strategy, the trade regime was strongly oriented towards import substitution and inward-looking. Moreover, it was one of the most centrally controlled sectors in the economy. The function of trade was to cover the gaps in the economy. The importation of 156 programmes from the former Soviet Union in the 1950s and several complete plants, mainly from Japan, in the 1960s and 1970s helped to establish certain industries such as steel, machinery, and chemicals in China. However, except perhaps for the 156 programmes, other imports, though most of them were capital goods, had never played an important role in China's industrial development. Trade in the pre-reform period played a relatively negligible role in the economy as a whole. Broadly speaking, imports were necessary to cover shortages of domestic supply, and exports were encouraged only to earn the necessary foreign exchange and to keep international payments balanced.

China's trade policy reforms have been carried out as a part of the general economic reforms since 1978, when the national economy was on the verge of collapse. The overall economic reforms originated in rural areas in agriculture, in the form of a household responsibility system. When this gradually turned out to be a success, reforms were also carried out in urban areas in other sectors, but on an experimental

[1] I am grateful to the Royal Institute of International Affairs for its financial support for this research. I am also grateful to Mr David Wall, who kindly provided some of the materials for the research and made very useful comments. Of course, the author alone is responsible for any errors in the paper.

basis. It was not until 1984, when the Central Committee of the Chinese Communist Party passed a resolution on reforms of China's economic system, that the reforms were formally implemented.[2] In its resolution, the Party affirmed the achievements in rural reforms, assessed the experiments in urban reforms, and declared that the conditions were ripe for an overall reform of the economic system.

In accordance with the resolution, urban reforms were carried out in a comprehensive way, involving almost all the sectors, including prices, enterprise, the financial system and trade. The reforms were focused on decentralization and utilization of market mechanisms with the purpose of revitalizing enterprises, especially state-owned enterprises (SOEs): the emphasis was initially on price reform, and later also on enterprise reform. The central government tried to boost economic activities (1) by changing relative prices, with a special effort to raise the relatively low prices of raw materials and basic agricultural products, such as rice and cotton, and later by letting the prices of more and more goods be decided by market forces; and (2) by letting local governments (including provincial and lower levels) and enterprises have more autonomy. The price reform, though often accompanied by relatively high inflation, has been quite successful. The planned commodities, whose prices were controlled by the Ministry of Domestic Trade (the former Ministry of Commerce), were reduced from 274 categories in 1978 to only 12 categories in 1992. As of 1993, 85 per cent of agricultural and sideline products and 95 per cent of manufactured goods were left to market adjustment.[3] However, the prices of factors of production, especially interest rates and wage rates, are still not freely determined by the market. On the other hand, the enterprise reform, by allowing the development of non-state-owned enterprises and granting autonomous rights to SOEs, has given their market activities a shot in the arm. The SOEs, which still make up a major part of the economy, are not yet efficient enough to survive market competition after many years of attempts in various kinds of reform measures.

---

[2] 'Resolution of the Chinese Communist Party on the Reform of Economic System', 20 October 1984 (pamphlet in Chinese).
[3] Sun, 1994.

External trade has played an increasingly important role in China's economy, so trade policy reforms have not only been an important component of the general economic reforms, but have also exerted a greater impact on China's economic development, especially on the development of trade and industry. This paper focuses on the impact of trade policy reforms on China's trade structure and industrial development. The next chapter gives a brief sketch of the trade policy reforms since 1979. Chapter 3 discusses the development and changing pattern of trade in China. Chapter 4 focuses on the impact of trade policy reforms on the development of industry. The final chapter draws some tentative conclusions.

# 12 TRADE POLICY REFORMS SINCE 1979

As an important aspect of the opening-up policy, foreign trade was required to play a more active role in the whole economy, so that reforms in the external sector were also regarded as an important part of the overall economic reforms. Like other sectors of reforms in the urban area, trade policy reforms were not formally implemented until 1984. These can be roughly divided into three stages: pre-1987; between 1988 and 1991; and the years after 1991.

## The first stage of reform

The trade policy reforms before 1987, said to be at 'an experimental stage', were characterized by decentralization of administrative control. The key step was to change the mandatory planning system into a combination of command plans, guidance plans and market mechanisms. Before 1979, the state decided on procurement plans for over 3,000 products for export, and directly arranged for the import of over 90 per cent of import orders. Since 1979, the range the command plan covered was gradually reduced. As of 1985, there were only about 100 product categories under the state command plan with quantitative export targets. There were also about 100 product categories under the guidance plan which only set targets of total export value for them.[4] The rest of the products were left for the market. But according to an estimate, in 1986, there were still 60 per cent of exports and 40 per cent of imports subject to the mandatory plan, and 20 per cent of exports and 30 per cent of imports subject to the guidance plan.[5] Therefore, the imports and exports actually determined by the market were still quite limited during this period.

---

[4] Yin, 1993.

[5] World Bank, 1993, pp. 10–25.

Together with this reform of the mandatory planning system, rights to engage in foreign trade business were also decentralized. Previously, there were only twelve specialized national import and export companies engaged in foreign trade. When the reforms started, provinces and ministries (other than the Ministry of Foreign Economic Relations and Trade, MOFERT) were gradually allowed to establish their own import and export companies. The number of tradables formerly controlled by the twelve specialized national import and export companies was reduced. Some large and medium-sized manufacturing enterprises with better equipment and technology and experienced in producing goods for export were also granted certain trading rights. Guangdong and Fujian Provinces, with their four special economic zones, were granted special preferential policies in foreign trade and foreign investment.

At the same time, various measures were introduced to promote and regulate foreign trade:

(1) *Licences and tariffs* A system of import and export licensing was introduced in 1980 to control the volume and range of commodities being traded. The range of commodities for which licences were required was initially small, but gradually expanded as the scope of planning departments shrank. It was estimated that by 1987 there were 45 categories of imports and 159 categories of exports subject to licensing. The reason why there were more exports than imports subject to licensing is that China wanted to monitor and control exports (mostly foodstuff) to Hong Kong and Macao. If licensed exports to Hong Kong and Macao were excluded, only 37 commodities required export licences.[6]

During the pre-reform years, as tariffs were not used as a major tool for influencing the volume and type of commodities traded under the central planning system, they were seldom adjusted. After 1980, however, tariff rates were more frequently adjusted to suit government trade policy. The general trend was for the level of tariff rates to increase in the first and second stages of the reforms and then decrease after 1992.

---

[6] Lardy, 1992.

(2) *Agency system* An agency system was introduced in 1984, and identified by MOFERT as a key factor in trade reform, and was also approved by the World Bank. In the early stages it was 'introduced to a very limited extent, probably covering less than 25 per cent of total trade thus far'.[7]

(3) *Trade subsidies* Export subsidies were given to those foreign trade companies which made losses in exporting their products because of domestic price distortion. When FTCs were required under export plans to purchase relatively high-priced domestic goods, such as certain types of machinery and electronic products, and then to sell them on the international market, they incurred financial losses. Likewise, they incurred losses when they were required by import policy to import such products as food grains and chemical fertilizers, which were purchased at international market prices, but then had to be sold on the domestic market at the state fixed price applicable to domestic producers of the same products. In 1987, the direct fiscal subsidies to FTCs to cover their losses were over Y28 billion.[8]

(4) *Tax rebates* The State Council formally approved a system of indirect tax rebates for exporters beginning in April 1985. China had several indirect taxes which were either levied directly on export goods or which affected the prices of export goods. However, since China's indirect tax structure, including a business tax, a product tax, and a value-added tax, was quite complicated, the administration of the tax rebate programme, which was based on a commodity-by-commodity investigation, was rather difficult. Despite its complexity, the size of rebates increased as the system evolved. In the first year, Y1.8 billion was rebated. By 1987, rebates had risen to Y7.4 billion.[9]

(5) *Foreign exchange retention system* Beginning in 1979, the central government gave up its monopoly on the control of foreign exchange by introducing a 'foreign exchange retention system', which allowed the export-producing firms, foreign trade companies and

---

[7] World Bank, 1988.

[8] World Bank, 1993.

[9] Zhou, 1990.

government administration to retain a certain percentage of the foreign exchange they earned from their exports. The proportion of retention quota to exports earnings varied between different regions and different enterprises. Although the quotas were also changed substantially over the years, they tended on the whole to expand rather than be reduced. For example, the rates for manufacturing firms under ministerial and local management in 1979 were 20 per cent and 40 per cent respectively of earnings above the level of 1978. By 1985, the rate for local authorities and enterprises was about 25 per cent of their planned export earnings. But the rate for FIEs in SEZs, enterprises in Tibet and for the PLA was 100 per cent.[10] Before 1988, retention quotas were transferable among enterprises only at the administrated exchange rate.

(6) *Dual exchange-rate system* China's foreign exchange rate had been overvalued for a long time, but was moving towards a gradual depreciation of the official rate while a *de facto* dual exchange rate system came into existence. In order to promote exports, an internal settlement rate of Y2.8 per US dollar for foreign trade was introduced against the official rate of about Y1.7 per dollar in 1981. This kind of dual rate was unified in 1984 when the official rate finally went down to Y2.8 per dollar. But in late 1986, dual exchange rates reappeared with the establishment of foreign exchange adjustment centres (FEACs). The rate determined in the FEACs was lower than the official rate, but before 1988 only state-owned foreign trade companies and enterprises with foreign trade rights (both domestic and foreign-invested) could enter this market. It was not until 1988 that all the foreign-invested enterprises and domestic enterprises with retention quotas were permitted to operate in the FEACs.[11]

In addition to the above-mentioned policy measures, China adopted several other export promotion measures, which included special programmes of enhanced export credits; preferential interest rates on domestic currency loans to firms producing for export; subsidized

---

[10] Fukasaku and Wall, 1994.

[11] World Bank, 1993, p. 30.

**Table 12.1: Foreign exchange reserves (US$ million)**

| Year | Government held foreign exchange | Year | Government held foreign exchange |
|------|--------------------------------|------|--------------------------------|
| 1980 | -1,296 | 1987 | 2,923 |
| 1981 | 2,708 | 1988 | 3,372 |
| 1982 | 6,986 | 1989 | 5,550 |
| 1983 | 8,901 | 1990 | 11,093 |
| 1984 | 8,220 | 1991 | 21,712 |
| 1985 | 2,644 | 1992 | 19,443 |
| 1986 | 2,072 | 1993 | 21,199 |

*Source: Statistical Yearbook of China 1994, p. 546.*

**Table 12.2: Losses of foreign trade corporations financed by central government budget (Y100 million)**

| Year | 1986 | 1987 | 1988 | 1989 | 1990 | 1991 |
|------|------|------|------|------|------|------|
| Losses | 249.6 | 282.1 | 268.5 | 336.4 | 224.4 | 176.1 |
| MEMO ITEM Total losses of SOEs within budget | 417.1 | 481.7 | 520.6 | 749.6 | 932.6 | 931.1 |

*Source: World Bank, 1993, p. 26.*

domestic transport, storage, and insurance of export goods and the development of manufacturing facilities devoted exclusively to export production. For example, there are export production bases where mostly agricultural and sideline products are made and processed.

Despite these various measures, imports and exports during the first stage of reform were still largely under central administrative control. Enterprises were not given much autonomy and their success in foreign trade was not great. The foreign exchange reserve did not increase proportionally with the growth of exports but decreased after 1984 (see Table 12.1), and the subsidies exerted a heavier burden on the central government (see Table 12.2). Thus, in 1988, the central government decided to extend the reforms to the management of foreign trade.

## The second stage of reform

The reforms undertaken between 1988 and 1991 were characterized by a change from direct planning control to the use of commercial policies such as tariffs and licences. One major reform measure was the implementation of a contract responsibility system to let producing firms and FTCs become more independent and more responsible for their losses and profits. Three targets were specified in the contracts: the amount of foreign exchange earnings; the amount of foreign exchange to be remitted to the central government; and a fixed amount of domestic currency that the centre would provide to subsidize losses on export sales.[12]

During this period, the command plans for both exports and imports were almost phased out. In the first quarter of 1992, only about 15 per cent of exports and 18.5 per cent of imports were subject to mandatory planning.[13] At the same time, other non-mandatory measures became increasingly important:

(1) *Tariffs and licences* As mentioned above, tariffs and licences were on the increase during this period. Calculated by the World Bank on the basis of the 1992 Harmonized System tariff schedule, the average unweighted tariff rate was 43 per cent, up 5 per cent from the corresponding average reported in 1986 and 4 per cent above the UNCTAD estimate of the unweighted average tariff rate in 1987. When weighted by the value of trade in each category (at world prices), the average tariff rate was 32 per cent, approximately 3 per cent above the 1987 UNCTAD estimate of 29 per cent. The tariff level would have been higher than computed were it not for (a) the sizeable reductions in tariff levels on 225 tariff lines implemented on 1 January 1992, and (b) the abolition, with effect from March 1992, of the Import Regulatory Duty.[14]

During the second period, the range of exports and imports covered by licences was also expanded. In the early 1988, there were

---

[12] World Bank, 1993, p. 26.

[13] World Bank, 1993, p. 28.

[14] World Bank, 1993, p. 48-9.

257 product categories covered by export licences. Though the number was reduced to 153 later, it rose again to 173 in 1989. There were also 53 product categories subject to import licensing in 1989.[15] Licenced trade accounted for two-thirds of all exports and 46 per cent of imports.[16]

However, in the case of China, although tariff rates and licences were generally on the increase during the 1980s, this should not be regarded as an increased barrier to trade, for two reasons. One is that there were still tariff reductions and exemptions, mainly for those materials and equipment imported for producing exports, and this accounted for a large part of China's imports (about 39 per cent in 1991). The other is that the increase of tariffs and licences took place at the time when the planning system was being phased out. The substitution of the mandatory plan with commercial policies is of course a big step towards international practice and market mechanisms in China's trade reforms. It is understandable that, in order to control the increasing amount of decentralized trade, the central government raised tariff rates and expanded licences while the plans were gradually being abolished. Therefore, the increase in the use of tariffs and licences can actually be seen as evidence of an improvement in China's foreign trade regime.

(2) *Agency system* The use of the agency system was asymmetric. From the late 1980s onwards, it was introduced rapidly and across a wide range of imports, covering almost all capital goods and about three-quarters of total imports by 1992. But it was only applied to about 10 per cent of total exports.[17]

(3) *Abolition of trade subsidies* Because of the heavy burden on trade subsidies, the central government fixed the amount of subsidies to national FTCs and provincial foreign trade administrative units in their contracts. As shown in Table 12.2, the total losses of FTCs financed by the central government reached their peak in 1989 at Y336.4 million, and then fell to Y176.1 million in 1991. By 1991,

---

[15] Yin, 1993.

[16] Lardy, 1992, p. 44.

[17] Fukasaku and Wall, 1994.

the central government decided formally to eliminate the subsidies. The purpose was of course to reduce its fiscal burden, which became heavier because of the overall losses made by SOEs. On the other hand, it also wanted the FTCs to be more responsible for their losses and profits.

(4) *Expansion of the retention scheme* In 1984/5, the foreign exchange retention rates for local authorities and enterprises were about 25 per cent of their planned export earnings. By 1988, however, corporations trading in priority sectors such as light industries, arts and crafts, clothing, machinery and electrical products, were permitted to retain between 70 and 100 per cent of foreign retention quotas.[18] At the same time, the retention rates that had been calculated by industry were eliminated to create a fairer competitive environment, as were the disparities that existed between different provinces, except Guangdong and Fujian, several of the autonomous regions populated by minority peoples, and the SEZs.

(5) *Expansion of the FEACs* FEACs were established all over the country during this period. By 1992, there were over 100 in operation. In addition to foreign-invested enterprises (FIEs), state-owned and collectively owned enterprises were also allowed to use FEACs, and quota controls on the utilization of retained foreign exchange were abolished in 1988. These measures led to significant increases in the volume of foreign currency transactions on secondary markets, from US$4.2 billion in 1987 to US$8.6 billion in 1989 and US$25 billion in 1992.

## The third stage of reforms

Trade policy reforms since 1991 were characterized by a lowering of trade barriers such as tariff rates and licences:

(1) *Reduction of tariff rates* On 1 January 1992, together with the implementation of a new Harmonized System tariff schedule, China reduced the import tariff rates on 225 tariff lines; on 1 March, it abolished the Import Regulatory Duty. On 31 December 1992,

---

[18] World Bank, 1993, p. 30.

import tariffs on 3,371 lines were again reduced, so that the general unweighted tariff level dropped from 42.8 per cent in 1991 to 39.9 per cent. At the end of 1993, import tariffs were further reduced on 2,898 lines. The unweighted tariff level fell to 36.4 per cent.[19]

(2) *Reduction of licensing control* Since 1993, the number of exports subject to licensing was reduced from 235 lines to 114 lines, and correspondingly the value of exports covered by licences was reduced from 60 per cent to about 30 per cent. The categorized (or canalized) exports were basically abolished. Except for 16 categories of exports[20] which were considered very important and which were still to be exported by designated FTCs, all the other exports were open to all the FTCs.[21]

On the import side, there were still 1,247 tariff lines subject to licensing and other forms of quantitative restriction as late as 1993. On 11 June 1994, restrictions on 195 tariff lines of importables were abolished. It was intended to reduce those subject to licensing by two-thirds within two years, and by the year 2000 to reduce those subject to quantitative restrictions by 1,000, from the present 1,274 lines to only about 240 lines.[22] At the same time, the rights to issue licences were further decentralized. In 1994, there were 143 categories of importables covered by licences, of which only 21 categories were subject to licences issued by MOFERT; licences of 59 categories were issued by the regional offices of MOFERT, and the remaining 63 categories were subject to provincial and municipal licensing.[23]

(3) *Reduction and adjustment of other controls* From 1992, the command plans for both exports and imports were abolished. It is claimed that the list of import substitution commodities was also abolished and

[19] Fan, 1994.

[20] The sixteen categories of exports are: rice, soybean, maize, tea, coal, tungsten, antimony, crude oil, refined oil, cotton, cotton yarn, cotton-polyester yarn, cotton grey, cotton-polyester grey, natural silk, and silk fabric.

[21] *Almanac of China's Foreign Economic Relations and Trade*, 1993, p. 50 (Chinese).

[22] *China's Foreign Trade*, No. 1, 1995 (Chinese).

[23] *China Customs*, No. 1, 1995 (Chinese).

the corresponding commercial credit was stopped.[24] From January 1994, imports were regulated according to the Provisional Method of Import Quota Regulation of General Commodities, the Provisional Method of Import Regulation of Machinery and Electronics Products, and the Provisional Method of Automatic Registration Regulation of Specific Commodities. All the importable machinery and electronics products are now subject to either quota or non-quota regulation. Those products subject to non-quota regulation are further divided into specific commodities and registered commodities. Importables subject to quota regulation and a specific commodity list have to be approved by the newly established State Council Machinery and Electronics Products Import and Export Office. Importables subject to registered commodity list can be imported automatically with only a registration at provincial level. In 1994, there were 196 tariff lines of imported machinery and electronics products covered by quota and 190 lines on the specific lists. Other machinery and electronics imports are subject to automatic registration, which is charged by ministerial and provincial authorities. For other general commodities, there are quota and specific lists. In 1994, there were 358 tariff lines of importables covered by quota and 361 tariff lines on the specific list. On the whole, importables covered by quota have been reduced by about one-fifth.[25]

(4) *Increase of transparency* Along with the improvement of the legal framework for foreign trade, the management of China's foreign trade has also become more open. China has published 347 documents about trade regulations and repealed 122. The above-mentioned three methods are published together with the list of specific commodities and commodities covered by the quotas. Commodities subject to licensing and the licence application procedure are also published in the national press; auctions of quotas have been tried out; tenders are invited on some large import pro-

---

[24] *Almanac of China's Foreign Economic Relations and Trade*, 1993, p. 51 and Li Lanqing on the 'Journalist Reception of the First Conference of the Eighth National Congress', *People's Daily*, 19 March 1993 (Chinese).

[25] Guo, 1994.

jects. In 1994, tenders were invited for 13 categories of commodities which were subject to licence regulation, and this number increased to 24 in 1995.[26]

In 1994, the trade law was published in an English version. According to Wu Yi, Minister at the Ministry of Foreign Trade and Economic Cooperation (MOFTEC, the former MOFERT), China was committed to continuing to improve the investment environment and to create conditions to let foreign business enjoy national treatment. China would also establish a relatively complete structure of laws and regulations on foreign trade and investment activities within about three years.[27]

Because of the further reductions of tariff rates and quantitative restrictions, the general level of trade protectionism has gone down. Though it is obviously still higher than the world standard, it is much lower than the previous level. And it should again be pointed out that the change from administrative planning control to commercial policy adjustment constitutes major progress in China.

(5) *Unification of exchange-rate system* The unification of the dual exchange-rate system, with effect from 1 January 1994, was considered a significant reform measure. With the unification of the exchange-rate system, the retention system was abolished, and enterprises now sell foreign exchange earned from export directly to the Bank of China at the listed prices. They can, by providing valid documents, buy foreign exchange for imports at the listed price. At the same time, a China Foreign Exchange Trade System was established in April 1994, with its centre in Shanghai, and most of the FEACs were closed.[28] The System deals with interbank foreign exchange trading and acts as agent for foreign-invested enterprises. So, as a transitional measure, FIEs can still keep their current account of foreign exchange without selling foreign exchange to the Bank of China at a spot price.

---

[26] *China's Customs*, No. 1, 1995 (a list of the 24 commodities can be found on page 35) (Chinese).

[27] Wu Yi, 'On the Basic Ideas of China's Foreign Economic Development in the 1990s', *China Foreign Trade*, No. 10, 1994 (Chinese).

[28] In some areas, there are still a few FEACs in existence.

# 13 TRADE POLICY REFORMS AND TRADE PERFORMANCE

Trade policy reforms have no doubt affected trade performance. China's trade performance since 1979 has in general been very good, much better than most other developing countries and of course better than its own performance in the thirty years before 1979. This, to a large extent, can be attributed to trade reforms, but other factors, such as reform in other sectors, the rise of FIEs and township and village enterprises (TVEs), etc., have also contributed to its success. A detailed quantitative analysis is not attempted here, but certain points can still be summarised.

## Trade growth

Table 13.1 shows that China's trade increased rapidly between 1978 and 1994, with an average annual growth rate of 17.05 per cent, much higher than the real growth of GNP. The average growth rates for exports and imports are 16.95 per cent and 17.24 per cent respectively per annum. From Table 13.2, we can see that, because of the faster growth of trade, the proportion of foreign trade to GNP has increased rapidly from less than 10 per cent in 1979 to 45 per cent in 1994, and the share of exports has risen from less than 5 per cent to about 23 per cent. Because of the rapid growth of foreign trade, China's ranking in world trade also rose from 36 in 1978 to 11 in 1993. By comparing the two tables, we can see that there were fluctuations in both economic growth and trade growth during these years. It is clear that the fluctuations in trade were synchronized with the movement of the whole economy. This indicates that trade performance is a part of the economic cycle and is largely affected by those factors that influence economic performance as a whole, such as macroeconomic policies. When the economy was overheated, trade also increased very fast. This

## Table 13.1: Trade performance in China (US$ billion)

| Year | Total export and import | Annual increase (%) | Total exports | Annual increase (%) | Total imports | Annual increase (%) | Balance of trade |
|------|------------------------|---------------------|---------------|---------------------|---------------|---------------------|------------------|
| 1978 | 20.64  |       | 9.75   |      | 10.89  |       | −1.14  |
| 1979 | 29.33  | 42.1  | 13.66  | 40.1 | 15.67  | 43.9  | −2.01  |
| 1980 | 38.14  | 30.1  | 18.12  | 32.7 | 20.02  | 27.8  | −1.90  |
| 1981 | 44.03  | 15.4  | 22.01  | 21.5 | 22.02  | 10.0  | −0.01  |
| 1982 | 41.61  | −5.5  | 22.32  | 1.4  | 19.29  | −12.4 | 3.04   |
| 1983 | 43.61  | 4.8   | 22.23  | −0.4 | 21.39  | 10.9  | 0.84   |
| 1984 | 53.55  | 22.8  | 26.14  | 17.6 | 27.41  | 28.1  | −1.27  |
| 1985 | 69.60  | 30.0  | 27.35  | 4.6  | 42.25  | 54.1  | −14.90 |
| 1986 | 73.85  | 6.1   | 30.94  | 13.1 | 42.90  | 1.5   | −11.96 |
| 1987 | 82.65  | 11.9  | 39.44  | 27.5 | 43.22  | 0.7   | −3.78  |
| 1988 | 102.79 | 24.4  | 47.52  | 20.5 | 55.28  | 27.9  | −7.76  |
| 1989 | 111.68 | 8.6   | 52.54  | 10.6 | 59.14  | 7.0   | −6.60  |
| 1990 | 115.44 | 3.4   | 62.09  | 18.2 | 53.35  | −9.8  | 8.75   |
| 1991 | 135.70 | 17.6  | 71.84  | 15.7 | 63.79  | 19.6  | 8.12   |
| 1992 | 165.53 | 22.0  | 84.94  | 18.2 | 80.59  | 26.3  | 4.35   |
| 1993 | 195.71 | 18.2  | 91.76  | 8.0  | 103.95 | 29.0  | −12.19 |
| 1994 | 236.70 | 20.9  | 121.00 | 31.9 | 115.70 | 11.3  | 5.30   |

*Source: Statistical Yearbook of China 1990, 1994* (Chinese); Statistical Bulletin on National Economic & Social Development 1994, *People's Daily*, 1 March 1995 (Chinese).

can be seen in 1984/5, 1987/8, and 1992/3. When economic growth slowed down, trade growth also slowed down, and even became negative. This can be seen in 1982/3, 1986, and 1989/90. Another notable feature is that, in the years in which the economy was overheated, imports increased much more quickly than exports, resulting in trade deficits. This typically reflects the phenomenon of 'investment hunger', an over-expanded demand originating mainly from a 'soft budget constraint'. But when retrenchment policies were implemented, imports dropped more dramatically than exports, indicating that imports are more affected by domestic demand, especially investment demand.

It should be pointed out that China saw trade deficits in most years after 1978. This is not because its exports increased at a slow rate, but because its fast economic growth produced high domestic demand for imported goods. Since China is a vast country with a potentially large

**Table 13.2: The ratio of foreign trade in China's GNP and its rank in world trade**

| Year | GNP (billion RMB Yuan) | Growth rate of GNP (%) | Real growth rate of GNP (%) | Ratio of total trade to GNP (%) | Ratio of exports to GNP (%)[a] | Rank of exports in world exports |
|------|------|------|------|------|------|------|
| 1978 | 358.81 | | | 9.89 | 4.67 | 36 |
| 1979 | 399.81 | 11.43 | 7.60 | 11.37 | 5.30 | — |
| 1980 | 447.00 | 11.80 | 7.80 | 12.75 | 5.69 | 26 |
| 1981 | 477.30 | 6.78 | 4.48 | 15.41 | 7.70 | 19 |
| 1982 | 519.30 | 8.80 | 8.75 | 14.85 | 7.79 | 17 |
| 1983 | 580.90 | 11.86 | 10.32 | 14.81 | 7.55 | 17 |
| 1984 | 696.20 | 19.85 | 14.58 | 17.25 | 8.34 | 18 |
| 1985 | 855.76 | 22.91 | 12.73 | 24.15 | 9.45 | 17 |
| 1986 | 969.63 | 13.30 | 8.31 | 26.61 | 11.16 | 16 |
| 1987 | 1,130.10 | 16.55 | 11.01 | 27.29 | 13.01 | 16 |
| 1988 | 1,406.82 | 24.49 | 10.98 | 27.17 | 12.56 | 16 |
| 1989 | 1,599.33 | 13.68 | 3.95 | 25.99 | 12.23 | 14 |
| 1990 | 1,769.53 | 10.64 | 4.99 | 31.42 | 16.87 | 15 |
| 1991 | 2,023.63 | 14.36 | 8.18 | 35.71 | 18.91 | 13 |
| 1992 | 2,437.89 | 20.47 | 13.22 | 37.42 | 19.18 | 11 |
| 1993 | 3,134.23 | 28.56 | 13.21 | 35.96 | 16.89 | 11 |
| 1994 | 4,380.00[b] | 39.75 | 11.80 | 45.66[c] | 23.34[c] | — |

[a] The ratios are calculated by the statistics of trade in renminbi, in the *Statistical Yearbook of China, 1994*, p. 506.
[b] GDP.
[c] Calculated by the exchange rate of Y8.45 per US$.
Source: *A Statistical Survey of China 1991* (Chinese); *Statistical Yearbook of China 1994* (Chinese); *Statistical Bulletin on National Economic & Social Development 1994* (Chinese).

domestic market, the effect of domestic demand on trade is much greater than the fluctuations in international markets. Therefore, only during a time of retrenchment, when domestic demand dropped, did the trade deficit diminish or disappear.

It should also be pointed out that trade development, especially the rapid increase of exports, has generally benefited from the trade policy reforms. Without the reforms, local government and enterprise initiatives would not have been instigated, and exports would not have increased so fast. However, the first wave of increases, between 1978

**Table 13.3: The export of primary goods and manufactured goods**

| Year | Total exports (US$ billion) | Primary goods (US$ billion) | Annual increase of primary exports (%) | Manufactures (US$ billion) | Annual increase of manufactures (%) | Share of manufactures in total exports (%) |
|------|------|------|------|------|------|------|
| 1980 | 18.119 | 9.114 | | 9.005 | | 49.7 |
| 1981 | 22.007 | 10.248 | 12.4 | 11.759 | 30.6 | 53.4 |
| 1982 | 22.321 | 10.050 | -1.9 | 12.271 | 4.4 | 55.0 |
| 1983 | 22.226 | 9.620 | -4.3 | 12.606 | 2.7 | 56.7 |
| 1984 | 26.139 | 11.934 | 24.1 | 14.205 | 12.7 | 54.3 |
| 1985 | 27.350 | 13.828 | 15.9 | 13.522 | -4.8 | 49.4 |
| 1986 | 30.942 | 11.772 | -14.9 | 19.670 | 45.7 | 63.6 |
| 1987 | 39.437 | 13.231 | 12.4 | 26.206 | 33.2 | 66.5 |
| 1988 | 47.516 | 14.406 | 8.9 | 33.110 | 26.3 | 69.7 |
| 1989 | 52.538 | 15.078 | 4.7 | 37.460 | 13.1 | 71.3 |
| 1990 | 62.019 | 15.886 | 5.4 | 46.205 | 23.3 | 74.4 |
| 1991 | 71.843 | 16.145 | 1.6 | 55.698 | 20.5 | 77.5 |
| 1992 | 84.940 | 16.989 | 5.2 | 67.951 | 22.0 | 80.0 |
| 1993 | 91.763 | 16.675 | -1.8 | 75.088 | 10.5 | 81.8 |
| 1994 | 121.000 | 19.670 | 18.0 | 101.330 | 34.9 | 83.7 |

*Source: Statistical Yearbook of China 1994.*

and 1981, cannot be attributed to the trade reforms, because they had not yet begun to take effect. Since the economy was on the verge of collapse in 1978, the increase in trade immediately afterwards was simply evidence of recovery, to be viewed alongside the recovery of the whole economy.

## Export of manufactured goods

Table 13.3 shows that, during the past fifteen years, China's export structure has also changed greatly, with a sharp rise in the proportion of manufactured goods in total exports. The share of manufactures in total exports increased from less than 50 per cent before 1980 to nearly 84 per cent in 1994. However, we can see from Table 13.3 that the rise of manufactured exports mainly took place in the second half of the 1980s. During the first half of the decade, the proportion of manfactures remained almost unchanged until it rose rapidly after 1985. There are several factors contributing to this phenomenon. One is, of course, the trade policy reforms. These started in the 1980s, but between 1981 and 1984, only a few experimental measures were implemented in some regions, such as Guangdong and the SEZs, and the measures implemented in the earlier years would take some time to become effective. It was not until 1984, when the resolution of the Party was enacted formally to start the reforms in the urban areas, that some important measures were taken in foreign trade reforms; these rapidly promoted China's exports, especially its manufactured exports.

The second factor is perhaps the sharp depreciation of the yuan from Y2.8 per dollar (the internal settlement rate of Y2.80 per dollar was introduced in 1981 and unified with the official rate in 1984) to Y3.20 and Y3.72 in 1985 and 1986. Since domestic prices were relatively high for manufactured goods and low for primary goods, compared with the world prices, the depreciation gave impetus to the export of manufactured products.

The third important factor is the inflow of foreign capital. However, this was not unique to China.[29] During the second half of the 1980s, there was an industrial restructuring in East and Southeast Asia with

---

[29] Fukasaku and Wall, 1994.

Japan and the four Little Dragons (Taiwan, Korea, Hong Kong and Singapore) moving relatively labour-intensive industries mainly to ASEAN countries and China. Like China, ASEAN countries, except perhaps the Philippines, took similar measures to reform their economy and attract foreign investment.

China did not use much foreign capital until the 1980s. During the early years of the 1980s, the actually utilized direct foreign investment was about US$442 million each year; this increased to US$1,959 million in 1985 and US$3,739 million in 1988.[30] Although the exact amount of foreign capital devoted to the production of exports is not known, most of the foreign capital in the early 1980s, which was directly linked to productive capacity in the mid-1980s, was in the form of relatively small investments, mainly from Hong Kong, in export-processing activities. For example, it was estimated that, by the end of 1990, there were 20,000 ventures engaged in processing exports in Guangdong alone, employing 1.37 million workers.[31]

The increase of processed exports and the rapid development of FIEs and TVEs also contributed to the fast increase of manufactured exports, which will be discussed below.

**Processed exports**

Processed exports were a new phenomenon developed along with the inflow of foreign direct investment and the rise of TVEs. Processed exports are not only an important factor contributing to the increase of manufactured exports, but are themselves also a distinctive feature of China's exports since 1978. There are generally two kinds of processed exports in China: those using supplied materials, and those using imported materials. From Table 13.4 we can see that processed exports also rose rapidly in the late 1980s, which corresponded to the rapid increase of manufactured exports. By 1994, the value of processed trade reached US$104.6 billion, accounting for 44.2 per cent of total trade, with processed exports of US$57 billion accounting for 47.1 per cent of China's total exports. Processed exports are mainly concentrated in

---

[30] National Statistical Bureau, *A Statistical Survey of China 1991*, p. 102 (Chinese).
[31] MOFERT, 1992.

**Table 13.4: Exports from assembly operations (US$ billion)**

| Year | 1988 | 1991 | 1993 | 1994 |
|------|------|------|------|------|
| 1. Exports processed with supplied materials | 6.5 | 12.9 | 16.0 | |
| 2. Exports processed with imported materials | 6.4 | 19.5 | 28.3 | |
| 3. Total value of processed exports | 12.9 | 32.4 | 44.3 | 57.0 |
| of which, from SEZs | 2.6 | 6.2 | | 8.0 |
| 4. Imports of materials for export processing | 13.7 | 25.0 | 36.4 | 47.6 |
| of which, from SEZs | 2.6 | 5.1 | | 6.3 |
| MEMO ITEM | | | | |
| Total merchandise exports | 47.5 | 71.8 | 91.8 | 121.0 |
| Total merchandise imports | 55.3 | 63.8 | 104.0 | 115.7 |

*Source*: World Bank: China Foreign Trade Reform: 'Meeting the Challenge of the 1990s', p. 12, Table 1.5; *China Customs*, No. 1 and No. 2, 1995.

coastal regions, with Guangdong alone accounting for about two-thirds of the total processed exports.[32]

The rapid increase of processed exports can also be seen in the two largest categories of China's exports: machinery and electronics, and light industrial products.[33] Before 1985, there were no statistics for processed exports in these two categories, but since 1985, they have increased rapidly. Table 13.5 shows that processed exports in 1985 accounted for 23.5 per cent of machinery and electronics exports. This figure rose to 32.3 per cent in 1988 and soared to 71.5 per cent in 1993.[34] At the same time, the share of processed exports in total light industrial exports also rose from 19.0 per cent in 1985 to 22.4 per cent in 1991. In China's largest export categories, processed exports have played a very important role. In 1993, they accounted for 52 per cent of total garment exports, 81.4 per cent of footwear exports, 94.5 per cent of toy exports, 28.3 per cent of textile exports, and 86.0 per cent of travel goods.[35]

---

[32] *China Customs*, No. 2, 1995.

[33] Since some of the machinery and electronics products are also light industrial goods, there is some overlap in the two categories.

[34] The figure for 1993 is taken from *China Customs*, No. 4, 1994.

[35] *China Customs*, No. 4, 1994.

**Table 13.5: Processed exports in machinery and electronics exports and in light industrial exports (US$10,000)**

| Year | Total value of mach. exports | Processed exports in mach. exports | Total value of light ind. exports | Processed exports in light ind. exports |
|------|------|------|------|------|
| 1984 | 221,761 | | 427,960 | |
| 1985 | 166,899 | 36,799 | 418,368 | 82,246 |
| 1986 | 248,154 | 66,347 | 534,665 | 114,916 |
| 1987 | 379,540 | 100,631 | 760,652 | 157,901 |
| 1988 | 615,881 | 196,424 | 997,388 | 219,738 |
| 1989 | 831,771 | 257,631 | 1,260,095 | 272,321 |
| 1990 | 1,108,820 | 298,544 | 1,556,338 | 349,682 |
| 1991 | 1,412,204 | 389,653 | 1,921,281 | 433,664 |

*Source: China Foreign Economic Statistics 1979–1991, pp. 162-4.*

With the rapid increase of processed exports, the imports for export processing also increased very quickly, since they can be exempted from import duties; by 1994 they accounted for 41.1 per cent of total imports.[36] This of course has much to do with reforms both of trade policies and of foreign investment policies. Without policy adjustment on import tariffs, such as the exemption from import duties of equipment and materials for export processing, processed exports would not have increased so fast. Likewise, without the encouragement of foreign investment, foreign businesses would not have become so actively involved in processed exports.

### The contribution of TVEs and FIEs

The rapid development of TVEs and FIEs has also made their contribution to foreign trade increasingly important. The contribution of these two kinds of enterprises to China's exports was negligible up to 1985, but since then has risen very quickly.

The contribution of TVEs to exports in 1985 was only about 4 per cent, but it rose to about one-third in 1993. The total foreign exchange

---

[36] *China Customs*, No. 2, 1995.

earned by TVEs in 1993 exceeded US$30 billion, about one-third of the total foreign exchange earnings that year. During the seventh five-year plan (1986–90), the delivered value of goods for export from TVEs increased by an average of Y10.5 billion each year, about one-third of the net increase in foreign exchange earnings; and between 1991 and 1993, the net additional value reached Y57.5 billion each year, about two-thirds of the net increase in foreign exchange earnings.[37]

Exports from FIEs rose even more quickly. Before 1987, these were negligible. In 1987, the exports from FIEs reached US$1.21 billion, accounting for 3.06 per cent of the total national exports. This increased to US$12 billion in 1991, accounting for 16.7 per cent of China's total exports.[38] In 1993, exports and imports of FIEs reached US$67.07 billion, accounting for 34.3 per cent of the country's total exports and imports, 7.9 per cent higher than in 1992. Exports from FIEs reached US$25.24 billion, accounting for 27.5 per cent of the country's total exports, 7.1 per cent higher than the previous year; imports reached US$418 billion, accounting for 40.2 per cent of the country's total imports, 7.5 per cent higher than the previous year. The trade of FIEs played a large part in China's trade deficit in 1993. However, if equipment and capital goods were excluded, the normal business imports of FIEs would only be US$25.2 billion, running a US$40 million surplus. The increase in trade of the FIEs contributed 8 percentage points to the total increase of trade in 1993. The increased value of exports from FIEs was US$7.88 billion, US$1.06 billion higher than the country's total increased export value of US$6.82 billion.[39] This means that the exports of other sectors, especially of SOEs, actually declined.

In 1993, the exports from TVEs and FIEs together accounted for over 60 per cent of China's total exports. The rise of TVEs and FIEs is no doubt one result of the general policy of reform and opening up. With the dismantling of the central planning system and the single

---

[37] *China's Township Enterprises*, No. 7, 1994 (Chinese).

[38] *China's Foreign-Invested Enterprises*, Jinghua Press, January 1994 (Chinese).

[39] The SEZ Office of the State Council, 'A Survey of Foreign Investment in 1993', *Foreign Investment in China*, No. 5, 1994.

## Table 13.6: Exports from special economic zones, US$100m (current prices)

| | Shenzhen | Shantou | Zhuhai | Xiamen | Hainan | China |
|---|---|---|---|---|---|---|
| **TOTAL EXPORTS** | | | | | | |
| 1981 | 0.2 | neg. | 0.1 | 1.4 | 0.5 | 220.0 |
| 1990 | 50.5 | 5.7 | 8.1 | 9.2 | 5.4 | 621.0 |
| 1991 | 56.0 | 8.2 | 11.1 | 12.7 | 6.7 | 719.0 |
| 1993 | 69.4 | 15.6 | 14.9 | 22.1 | 8.9 | 917.6 |
| **EXPORTS BY FFEs** | | | | | | |
| 1991 | 29.0 | 2.8 | 5.0 | 3.0 | 0.5 | 120.5 |
| As % of total 1991 | 51.7 | 34.5 | 45.6 | 24.0 | 8.5 | 16.8 |
| **EXPORTS BY MUNICIPAL FTCs** | | | | | | |
| 1991 | 9.7 | na | 3.3 | 6.2 | 4.6 | na |
| As % of total 1991 | 17.4 | | 41.0 | 50.0 | 73.0 | |
| **EXPORTS BY HINTERLAND FTCs** | | | | | | |
| 1991 | 1.8 | na | na | 2.2 | na | na |
| As % of total 1991 | 3.3 | | | 17.5 | | |

*Source*: David Wall, 'China's Special Economic Zones', Table 8; *Statistical Yearbook of China*, and *China Customs*, No. 4, 1994.

(public) ownership system, non–state–owned enterprises[40] developed rapidly. Preferential trade policies attracted these relatively independent enterprises to become involved in foreign trade activities.

## Exports from Special Economic Zones

A new feature in China's foreign trade after 1978 is the rapid growth of exports from the Special Economic Zones, which were successful in attracting foreign capital, production, foreign trade and overall economic development.[41] As shown in Table 13.6, the export growth was

---

[40] In China, non–state owned sectors include collectively owned enterprises, privately (individual) owned enterprises, foreign-invested enterprises, and joint ventures invested by both state-owned and collectively owned sectors, etc.

[41] For a detailed account of the performance of China's special economic zones, see David Wall, *China's Special Economic Zones*, a report prepared for the World Bank; and his section in this book.

remarkable and FIEs played a major role in their export performance. In 1994, the total trade of the SEZs reached US$33.35 billion, in which exports contributed US$16.94 billion. The FIE exports from SEZs in 1993 reached US$6.04 billion, accounting for 23.9 per cent of total FIE exports of the country. This figure again rose to US$6.18 billion in 1994.[42] The success of SEZs is largely due to the special policy privileges they have enjoyed. In foreign trade, for example, firms investing in SEZs have been exempted from import licences, and their exports are free of all duties and indirect taxes.[43]

## The role of Hong Kong

Hong Kong has always been an important 'bridge' connecting China with the rest of the world. Since the reform and opening-up, this role has been increasingly important, especially to the success of China's export drive. Hong Kong has always been China's biggest trade partner; and China has always been in a surplus position. In the mid-1980s, trade with Hong Kong accounted for about 18 per cent of China's total trade, with exports accounting for about 22 per cent and imports about 15 per cent. In 1991 and 1992, trade with Hong Kong rose to 36.6 per cent and 35.1 per cent respectively of China's total trade, in which exports accounted for 47.8 per cent and 44.2 per cent, and imports 27.4 per cent and 25.5 per cent.[44] Although the proportion of trade with Hong Kong to China's total trade again dropped to about 17 per cent in 1993,[45] Hong Kong was still China's largest trade partner. It was noted that more than half of China's exports to the rest of the world are handled by Hong Kong.[46]

More importantly, it is estimated that 70 per cent of the cumulative value of US$58.5 billion in foreign direct investment commitments to China has come from Hong Kong.[47] In 1985, China's total utilized for-

---

[42] *China Customs*, No. 2, 1995.

[43] Wall, 1993.

[44] *Almanac of China's Foreign Economic Relations and Trade*, 1986 and 1993.

[45] *Statistical Yearbook of China*, 1994.

[46] World Bank 1993, p. 15.

[47] World Bank, 1993, p. 15.

eign capital was US$4.46 billion, with foreign direct investment of US$1.96 billion. The corresponding figures from Hong Kong were US$1.02 billion and US$0.96 billion, accounting for 22.9 per cent and 49.0 per cent of the country's total. In 1993, the share of utilized capital from Hong Kong rose to 48.9 per cent and foreign direct investment rose to 62.8 per cent. It should be noted, however, that in China's FDI statistics, investment flows from Hong Kong and Macao include those by subsidiaries of foreign and Chinese firms located there.[48]

Not only has Hong Kong accounted for the largest share of China's foreign direct investment, but this investment has mostly been directed to export-oriented joint ventures and processing activities in the coastal provinces, Guangdong in particular. It is estimated that Guangdong has attracted about 50 per cent of the country's foreign investment commitment and accounted for almost 40 per cent of China's exports. Guangdong's share in processing exports is even larger.[49] In 1994, its export and import processing combined reached a total of US$65.7 billion, accounting for 62.8 per cent of China's total processing trade.[50] It is clear that the economies of Hong Kong and Guangdong have been increasingly integrated.

### The export of direct labour services

The export of direct labour services was negligible before 1978. Since the 1980s, this kind of export has also developed relatively fast. In 1985 the total value of contracted projects and labour service cooperation was US$1.3 billion. This had increased more than fourfold to US$6.8 billion by 1993. The number of persons working overseas increased from 56,264 to 130,984 by 1992.[51] However, compared with its commodity trade, the export of labour is still small and unimportant to China's economic development.

---

[48] Fukasaku and Wall, 1994.

[49] *Almanac of China's Foreign Economic Relations and Trade*, 1993.

[50] *China Customs*, No. 3, 1995.

[51] *Almanac of China's Foreign Economic Relations and Trade*, 1993 and *Statistical Yearbook of China*, 1994.

## Conclusion

In short, trade performance is affected by many factors. Trade policy reforms are of course the most direct and influential factor. On the one hand, with the process of decentralization, different provinces, regions and enterprises have been granted greater rights to carry on foreign trade. They are more actively involved in trade to earn more foreign exchange. On the other hand, measures for promoting exports and restricting/liberalizing imports, including tariffs, quotas, licences, subsidies, tax rebates, foreign exchange retention etc. not only directly promote exports, but also promote a change in the export structure. Without trade policy reforms, including exchange-rate reform, the initiatives of local governments and enterprises to export would not have been taken and exports would not have increased so fast.

Besides the trade policy reforms, however, there are also other factors affecting China's trade performance: in particular, macroeconomic policies and domestic economic fluctuations. The synchronization of trade growth and economic growth in the past sixteen years has demonstrated this, although their causal relations are still not very clear.

Enterprise reform, together with the rise of TVEs and FIEs, is another important factor. Because of the reform, enterprises became more responsible for their own losses and profits, and with the implementation of price reform, they became more sensitive to price changes. Thus, when given preferential treatment for exports, enterprises sought to export their products for more profit and foreign exchange. Of course, the SOEs are in general not very efficient and many of them still make losses, but the non-state sector, especially TVEs and FIEs, have developed rapidly and their contribution to the total trade volume has increased sharply.

There are also indirect factors such as price and other reforms. With the price reform, more and more prices are determined by the market. This makes it possible for the central government gradually to phase out subsidies for FTCs and manufacturing firms, and to liberalize trade policies, which in turn promote the development of trade. It is clear that, without price reform, it would not be possible to eliminate the mandatory import and export plans.[52]

---

[52] World Bank, 1993.

# 14 THE IMPACT OF TRADE POLICY REFORMS ON INDUSTRIAL DEVELOPMENT

## Industrial policy and trade policy

Industrial structure and industrial development are more directly affected by industrial policies. Broadly speaking, trade policy can be considered to be a part of industrial policy. In a narrow sense, however, industrial policy can be considered to be the policy that directly affects the progress and structural change of industry, especially manufacturing industry. In this sense, it is different from trade policy. China's industrial policy has been changed several times since 1949.

Before 1978, the focus of industrial policy was on heavy industries, such as iron and steel, machinery and equipment.[53] Between 1952 and 1978, the total output of heavy industries increased 40 times while the total output of light industries increased only 16 times.[54] Since 1978, however, with the implementation of the reform and opening-up policies, China's industrial policy has also changed. For the first time since 1949, the policy focus was turned onto light industries, and heavy industries were required to break out of their self-sufficient circle[55] and

---

[53] Heavy industries in China are defined by the State Statistical Bureau as those industries that produce means of production, which are further divided into (1) extraction industries; (2) raw material industries; and (3) processing industries. On the other hand, light industries are those which provide consumption goods and hand tools, which are further divided into (1) those which use agricultural products as materials; and (2) those which use non-agricultural products as materials.

[54] The Study Group of the Economic Institute, State Planning Commission, 'The problem of dual structure and the economic development in the 1990s' (in Chinese), *Economic Research*, No. 7, 1993.

[55] In China, heavy industry is used to produce products for its own use. For example, the iron and steel industry supplied its products to the machine tool industry and the machine tool industry produced equipment that the iron and steel industry

**Table 14.1: Change in share of light and heavy industries in total industrial output (%)**

| Year | 1978 | 1980 | 1985 | 1989 | 1990 | 1991 | 1992 | 1993 |
|---|---|---|---|---|---|---|---|---|
| Light industries | 43.1 | 47.2 | 47.4 | 48.9 | 49.4 | 48.9 | 47.2 | 44.0 |
| Heavy industries | 56.9 | 52.8 | 52.6 | 51.1 | 50.6 | 51.1 | 51.1 | 56.0 |

*Source: Statistical Yearbook of China's Industrial Economy 1993 and Statistical Yearbook of China 1994.*

to support the development of light industries and agriculture. And, also for the first time, the growth of light industries overtook that of heavy industries: between 1978 and 1990, the average annual growth rate of light industries was 14.0 per cent, while that of heavy industries was only 10.5 per cent.[56] However, the growth of heavy industries has accelerated in the 1990s. In 1991, 1992 and 1993, the growth rates of heavy industries were 19.29 per cent, 35.49 per cent and 50.75 per cent, while those of light industries were 16.83 per cent, 26.74 per cent and 32.54 per cent respectively,[57] indicating another change of industrial policy focus. Table 14.1 shows these fluctuations of light and heavy industries. It is clear that during the 1980s, the share of light industry in total industrial output increased, but it has again dropped since 1992.

Within the broad category of the so-called heavy industry, the emphasis has been shifted from large-scale, capital-intensive basic industries such as iron and steel, which are environment-polluting, to more technology- and knowledge-intensive, pollution-reducing industries, such as electronics, computers, office automation equipment, etc. In the early 1980s, the policy emphasis was still on iron and steel, which was reflected in the construction of the Baoshan Iron and Steel Plant in Shanghai in September 1981. But since the late 1980s, more empha-

---

needed, while light industry and the agricultural sector did not get an adequate supply of equipment and machinery, which accounts for their relatively slow growth.

[56] Calculated from data in the *Statistical Yearbook of China*, various issues.

[57] Calculated from *Statistical Yearbook of China* 1994, p. 377.

sis has been put on technology-intensive industries producing durable goods, petrochemicals, automobiles, etc and high-technology industries such as microelectronics, space technology, biotechnology engineering, etc. At the same time, a series of programmes to promote the development of high-tech industries was carried out; the most widely known is the Torch Programme, designed to bridge the gap between basic research and productive application of new technology achievements. In order to better implement this programme, 52 high-tech development zones at national level, and many more at provincial and regional levels, have been established. Enterprises involved in these activities, once certified as 'advanced technology enterprises',[58] can enjoy different kinds of preferential treatment, including import tariff reduction or exemption.

More recently, in a document entitled 'The Framework of National Industrial Policy for the 1990s', produced by the State Council on 25 March 1994, three kinds of industries are mentioned as priority industries: infrastructure and basic industries; leading (pillar) industries; new and high-technology industries. The encouragement of the development of the first sector comes about because basic industries and infrastructure have always been the bottleneck in China's economic development. The emphasis on the development of the latter two sectors obviously reflects China's eagerness to upgrade its industrial structure. Leading (pillar) industries are defined as machinery and electronics, petrochemicals, automobiles and construction. More detailed policy measures for these industries have been or will be drawn up. For example, as a part of this national industrial policy, the Planning Commission produced the national industrial policy for automobiles in February 1994. These leading sectors will be certain to receive preferential treatment to support their development.

Foreign trade policy in China is regarded as supplementary to industrial policy. One of its major objectives is to stimulate the upgrad-

---

[58] This status requires: (1) investing in industries or projects that are encouraged by the state; (2) using internationally advanced or adequate techniques and equipment; and (3) an agreement regarding technology transfer, or a clause regarding technology transfer in the investment contract.

ing of technology and the development of new industries.[59] In the 'Framework' document, the enterprises to be encouraged to export are those producing agricultural and sideline products, light industrial products and textiles with comparative advantage; domestically produced durable goods and other machinery and electronics with mature technology; products with high added value and international competitiveness; and high-technology products. It is also stipulated that the state encourages the importation of new technology and related key equipment, key components and parts; the expansion of imports of primary products that are in short supply in China; and the acceleration of the process of importing and absorbing new technology by infant industries to produce new equipment and key components and parts.

It is clear that the major function of export policy is to generate as much foreign exchange as possible, which is also reflected in the foreign exchange earning targets set for FICs by the Ministry of Foreign Trade and Economic Cooperation (MOFTEC, formerly MOFERT). Therefore, except for a few products such as cereals, coal, cotton, etc., almost any item can enjoy export promotion treatment as long as it is for export. But more recently, with the enacting of the 'Framework', export policy seems to be required to coordinate more closely with industrial policy. MOFTEC has set the objectives for promoting exports: supporting and developing exports with high-tech contents and high added value to turn technology-intensive industries into leading export industries. The focus will be on machinery and electronics products, chemicals and metallurgical products, etc., with machinery and electronics as the most important exports, in the hope that they will become the largest category of exports, reaching a target value of US$60 billion by the year 2000.[60] To realize this objective, an import-export bank has been set up to support the export of machinery and electronics products.

The function of import policy is more directly related to the upgrading of the industrial structure. First, although the general level of tariff rates has been reduced, the tariff structure is more or less the same

---

[59] World Bank, 1993.
[60] Ming, 1995.

as it was in 1991 and is similar to other developing countries, which ensures that finished goods are more protected than upstream inputs. For example, in the tariff reduction of 31 December 1992, the focus was on four kinds of products: (1) raw materials that China needs to import in the long run; (2) advanced technology products that China is not able to produce; (3) several products from other developing countries; and (4) manufactures for which China is competitive in international markets. One of the major principles underlying this is that the degree of reduction should be determined according to industrial policy, so that, for example, imports of equipment with advanced technology and raw materials in short supply were encouraged. In addition, certain necessities also enjoyed larger reductions.[61] On 31 December 1993, the tariff rates for some raw materials and equipment were further reduced; and perhaps because of the pressure from the international community, rates for some agricultural products and finished manufactures such as refrigerators, microwave ovens, television sets, etc. were also reduced.[62]

Second, since there are various kinds of exemptions, the tariff revenue from imports is relatively low compared with other developing countries, and resembles more the situation in developed countries. The largest categories of import duty exemptions have been for materials used for export processing with supplied materials and export processing with imported materials, which consisted of 77.8 per cent of total concessional imports in 1991. The next two largest categories are the equipment imported with foreign investment, which comprised 14.6 per cent of total concessional imports, and the equipment for processing supplied materials, comprising 2.8 per cent of total concessional imports.[63] This shows that the function of tariffs in China is mainly for protection rather than duty collection, but exports and foreign investment, which is encouraged for either producing exports or relatively technology-intensive products, are favoured by the import policy.

Third, as for non-tariff barriers (NTBs), there are three objectives: allocating a fixed quantity of planned imports between users; protec-

[61] *China Customs*, No. 1, 1993.

[62] *China Customs*, No. 12, 1993.

[63] World Bank, 1993.

tion; and balance of payments control. Since the command plan has been abolished and the domestic prices of commodities have been mostly liberalized, the first objective is not important nowadays. It is also very difficult to distinguish when import licensing or controls are used for balance of payments purposes and when they are not. Therefore, NTBs are also mainly used for the purpose of protection whose coverage is high where tariffs are high.[64] For example, the quota list for machinery and electronics in 1994 mainly included finished goods and key components such as automobiles and engines, colour TV and cathode ray tubes, refrigerators and compressors, etc. And the quota list for general commodities mainly included raw materials, tobacco, alcohol and soft drinks.[65]

Although trade policy is required to support industrial policy for the purpose of upgrading technology and developing new industries, and has to a certain extent succeeded in doing so, the two kinds of policies cannot be said to be well coordinated. This is because, on the one hand, they are drawn up by different departments of the State Council, with different perspectives and different interests; and, on the other hand, while trade policy necessarily requires a national perspective, industrial policy has become very much a provincial concern.[66] The establishment of the State Council Economic and Trade Commission and the enacting of the 'Framework of National Industrial Policy for the 1990s' are important attempts at better coordination of trade policy and industrial policy.

### Exports and industrial development

As mentioned above, China has taken various measures to promote the development of exports. The most important of these are different kinds of preferential tax treatment, such as tax rebates and tax holidays for export enterprises, and foreign exchange retention (before 1994). Since FIEs can keep current accounts for their foreign exchange, they did not need any 'retention'. Moreover, once they are certified as

---

[64] World Bank, 1993, p. 66-7.
[65] *China Customs* No. 4, 1994 and No. 2, 1995.
[66] World Bank, 1993, p. 103.

Table 14.2: The value and share of various types of products in China's manufactured exports: selected years 1965–1990

| Product category | 1965 | 1975 | 1980 | 1985 | 1990 | Growth rate (%) | |
| --- | --- | --- | --- | --- | --- | --- | --- |
| | | | | | | 1965–90 | 1980–90 |
| *Value of China's exports ($m)* | | | | | | | |
| TOTAL EXPORTS | 1,718 | 6,303 | 18,237 | 27,764 | 80,541 | 16.6 | 16.0 |
| Labour-intensive manufactures | 570 | 2,253 | 7,168 | 12,319 | 59,787 | 20.5 | 23.6 |
| Unskilled labour-intensive goods | 454 | 1,557 | 5,254 | 9,742 | 41,222 | 19.8 | 22.9 |
| Capital-intensive manufactures | 1,113 | 3,128 | 6,353 | 7,984 | 14,978 | 10.9 | 8.9 |
| Human capital-intensive goods | 148 | 473 | 1,292 | 1,708 | 12,325 | 19.3 | 25.3 |
| Natural resource-based products | 961 | 3,665 | 9,116 | 13,339 | 16,585 | 12.1 | 6.2 |
| Coal, petroleum and gas | 32 | 897 | 3,974 | 7,157 | 5,290 | 22.7 | 2.9 |
| *As a share of total exports (%)* | | | | | | | |
| TOTAL EXPORTS | 100 | 100 | 100 | 100 | 100 | — | — |
| Labour-intensive manufactures | 33 | 36 | 39 | 44 | 74 | — | — |
| Unskilled labour-intensive goods | 26 | 25 | 29 | 35 | 51 | — | — |
| Capital-intensive manufactures | 65 | 50 | 35 | 29 | 19 | — | — |
| Human capital-intensive goods | 9 | 8 | 7 | 6 | 15 | — | — |
| Natural resource-based products | 56 | 58 | 50 | 48 | 21 | — | — |
| Coal, petroleum and gas | 2 | 14 | 22 | 26 | 7 | — | — |

*Source:* World Bank, 1993, p. 9.

'export enterprises',[67] they can enjoy preferential treatment. For example, at the end of the income exemption and reduction period, an export enterprise whose exports reach 70 per cent of its total output can still enjoy a 50 per cent reduction of income tax; export enterprises in SEZs and in ETDZs can enjoy a preferential income tax rate – 10 per cent rather than 15 per cent.[68] Although with preferential treatment the price of some export products might be lower than their prices on the domestic market, this does not guarantee their export. The ability to export depends on comparative advantage and the competitiveness of the products. Therefore, with the reduction of export controls, there was a kind of comparative advantage effect. When the preferential export policy measures were implemented, they would take effect on those goods that have comparative advantage and potential competitiveness. It is obvious that the biggest advantage for China is its abundant labour resource and its relatively low wage rate. This explains why the labour-intensive processed exports have increased most quickly, and even within the category of machinery and electronics products, a large proportion is processed exports. It is quite clear that these goods themselves may be capital- and technology-intensive, but assembly activities in China are still labour-intensive. This also explains why the exports of manufactures during the past twenty-five years or so have changed from relatively capital-intensive to relatively labour-intensive.

Table 14.2 is taken from World Bank estimates. It shows that the share of labour-intensive exports in total exports rose from 33 per cent in 1965 to 74 per cent in 1990, while the share of capital-intensive goods decreased from 65 per cent to 19 per cent. This change of export structure did not reflect a change in China's comparative advantage from capital-intensive products to labour-intensive products. It is merely that, under the central planning regime, exports did not reflect the comparative advantage of China, but were the products of mandatory

---

[67] The title of 'export enterprises' is granted if a foreign-invested enterprise exports 70 per cent or more of its total annual output; or if it exports 50 per cent or more and can keep its foreign exchange income and expenditure balanced.

[68] For more detailed information, see the Stipulation of the State Council on Encouragement of Foreign Investment, 11 October 1986.

plans and reflected the focus of industrial policies. Since the production structure was biased toward relatively capital-intensive heavy industries, relatively capital-intensive products were exported. They could be sold on the international market at very low prices, even lower than their real costs, in order to earn the necessary foreign exchange. But with the progress of reform, when enterprises were gradually allowed to take responsibility for their own business and the market began to play an increasingly important role, competition forced enterprises to export those products in which they had comparative advantage and competitiveness.

While the export structure has actually turned to a relatively more labour-intensive one, reflecting China's comparative advantage, the change of industrial structure is unfortunately not very clear because of the lack of corresponding statistics. According to a World Bank estimate, China's industrial structure has remained almost unchanged.[69] However, there are still several points to be made. First, there are some statistical problems. One is that the gross value of industrial output (GVIO) shares in the World Bank report only pertain to output of firms with independent accounting, which accounted for 77.8 per cent of total GVIO in 1990. If all the firms were included, the situation might be different.

Another, more important, problem is that the total GVIO in China's statistics may not include all the industrial output produced by TVEs. The figures in Table 14.3 are taken from the same statistical yearbook. They show that TVEs' contribution to total GVIO in 1993 accounted for 44.5 per cent, almost the sum of both collective- and individual-owned enterprises (see Table 14.6), which is impossible because not all the collective- and individual-owned enterprises are TVEs. Table 14.3 also shows that in 1993 the number of employees working in TVEs involved in industrial production was greater than that of the national total in industrial production, which is also impossible. Therefore, the only explanation is that the national GVIO did not include all the output produced by TVEs. According to the figures in Table 14.3, we see that TVEs are much more labour-intensive. The value created by TVEs

---

[69] World Bank, 1993, Table 1.12 and Table A3.3.

**Table 14.3: Value of industrial output and number of employees in industry (Y100 million; 10,000 persons)**

| Year | Total value of industrial output | Total number employed in industry | Value of industrial output by TVEs | Total number employed by TVEs in industry |
|------|------|------|------|------|
| 1980 | 515.43 | | 50.94 | 1,942 |
| 1985 | 971.65 | 5,557 | 182.72 | 4,137 |
| 1986 | 1,119.42 | | 241.34 | 4,762 |
| 1987 | 1,381.30 | | 324.29 | 5,267 |
| 1988 | 1,822.91 | | 452.94 | 5,703 |
| 1989 | 2,203.41 | | 524.41 | 5,624 |
| 1990 | 2,392.44 | 6,378 | 605.03 | 5,572 |
| 1991 | 2,770.81 | 6,551 | 870.86 | 5,814 |
| 1992 | 3,706.58 | 6,621 | 1,363.54 | 6,336 |
| 1993 | 5,269.21 | 6,626 | 2,344.66 | 7,260 |

Source: *Statistical Yearbook of China 1994.*

in 1980 was Y2,623 per person/year, which increased to Y4,417 in 1985 and Y32,297 in 1993. But the average value of per person/year in the whole national industry was Y17,485 in 1985 and Y79,523 in 1993. If all the employees in TVEs were taken into consideration, the industrial structure could become relatively more labour-intensive.

Second, the TVEs' contribution to exports has increased quite quickly, and the share of export production in their total industrial production has also increased. In 1985, the value of exports accounted for about 6.9 per cent of their GVIO, and this increased to about 10 per cent in 1993.[70] This, on the one hand, indicates that exports have become more important in TVEs' industrial production, but on the other hand it still shows that TVEs are mostly domestically oriented. If we accept the assumption that most TVEs are labour-intensive, the rapid growth of labour-intensive TVEs for domestic production actually indicates a shift of industrial structure towards a relatively greater labour intensity, which reflects China's comparative advantage and corresponds to its export structure.

---

[70] The figure of export value for 1985 is taken from World Bank 1993 p. 14, and the figure for 1993 is taken from *China's Township Enterprises*, No. 7, 1994.

Third, even if we admit that the domestic industrial structure has remained almost unchanged, this does not mean that the relatively labour-intensive industries have not expanded, but only that the state has put much more effort into developing relatively capital- and technology-intensive industries, which has offset the expansion of labour-intensive industries.

Fourth, even if the domestic industrial structure has not been much affected by the change in the export structure, the expansion of labour-intensive production for exports both from FIEs and TVEs, and the rapid growth of TVEs in general industrial production, have no doubt promoted the industrialization of rural areas and provided many employment opportunities. This is most evident in the Zhujiang Delta region in Guangdong Province, the southern part of Jiangshu Province, and the Jiaodong Peninsula of Shandong Province.

Fifth, we should also note that since an increasing part of exports is accounted for by processed exports, the value added in exports has been small and the direct effect of exports on industrial development is not large. Moreover, the efficiency of processed exports seems to be decreasing in recent years. The import/export ratios[71] for processed exports between 1991 and 1994 are 1:1.30, 1:1.26, 1:1.22, and 1:1.198 respectively.[72]

**Imports and industrial development**

Imports in China are more directly linked with industrial development. An obvious change in the import structure is that the share of capital goods in imports has increased and that of intermediates has declined (see Table 14.4). This import structure, as the World Bank report pointed-ed out, reflects a conscious import strategy, which has been to ensure the supply of key raw materials and to acquire integral technology through the import of capital goods.[73]

With the deepening of trade policy reforms, China's import regime has also been gradually liberalized, at least in relation to the situation

---

[71] The ratio of value of imported materials used for exports to the value of exports.

[72] Statistical Information, *China Customs*, No. 4, 1994 and No. 2, 1995.

[73] World Bank, 1993, p. 17.

**Table 14.4: Import structure (% share of total)**

| Commodity | 1984 | 1987 | 1988 | 1989 | 1990 |
|---|---|---|---|---|---|
| Food | 9.8 | 7.2 | 7.7 | 9.1 | 8.6 |
| Mineral fuels | 0.5 | 1.2 | 1.4 | 2.8 | 2.4 |
| Intermediate | 53.8 | 43.2 | 46.1 | 43.1 | 39.4 |
| Consumer goods | 2.3 | 4.5 | 4.1 | 3.7 | 4.7 |
| Capital goods | 33.5 | 43.5 | 40.1 | 41.0 | 44.3 |
| Miscellaneous | 0.0 | 0.4 | 0.6 | 0.4 | 0.5 |

*Source:* World Bank 1993, p. 16.

that prevailed earlier, though probably not in comparison with other developing countries. However, it should not be denied that one of the main purposes of the import regime is to protect domestic industry and domestic market. With the import protection and other domestic preferential measures, such as tax exemption and reduction, preferential land-leasing terms, low-interest loans, etc., resources, including some foreign direct investment, have been drawn to some relatively technology-intensive industries. Some new industries, such as electronics, automobiles and durable goods, have been established and new products developed and sold in domestic markets instead of being imported. A process of import substitution has taken place especially in durable goods such as washing machines, television sets, refrigerators, etc. Although there is no breakdown of statistics for different industries in total industrial output by value, we can still see the growth of new industries by quantity. Table 14.5 presents the growth of production of some durable goods, and demonstrates the speed of growth compared with the overall industrial growth.

Since the protective structure in China favours the assembly process, a striking phenomenon is that such a high proportion of domestic resources and foreign investment has been drawn to the downstream assembly sector, while relatively fewer resources have been allocated to the production of intermediates – parts and components, machinery and equipment, and some materials – because they are relatively cheaper to import.

**Table 14.5: The development of some new industries (10,000 units)**

| Year | Household refrigerators | Household washing machines | Video recorders | Television sets | Of which: colour TV sets |
|------|------------------------|---------------------------|-----------------|-----------------|--------------------------|
| 1980 | 4.9   | 24.5    | 74.3    | 249.2   | 3.2      |
| 1985 | 144.8 | 887.2   | 1,393.1 | 1,667.7 | 435.3    |
| 1986 | 225.0 | 893.4   | 1,756.8 | 1,459.4 | 414.6    |
| 1987 | 401.3 | 990.2   | 1,978.0 | 1,934.4 | 672.7    |
| 1988 | 757.6 | 1,046.8 | 2,540.4 | 2,505.1 | 1,037.66 |
| 1989 | 670.8 | 825.4   | 2,349.0 | 2,766.5 | 940.0    |
| 1990 | 463.1 | 662.7   | 3,023.5 | 2,684.7 | 1,033.0  |
| 1991 | 469.9 | 687.2   | 2,873.7 | 2,691.4 | 1,205.1  |
| 1992 | 485.8 | 707.9   | 3,231.8 | 2,867.8 | 1,333.1  |
| 1993 | 596.7 | 895.9   | 3,647.9 | 3,033.0 | 1,435.8  |

Source: *Statistical Yearbook of China 1994.*

Because of the tariff exemption and other preferential treatment, repeated imports of the same production lines have been a frequent occurrence in China. For example, it was reported that different provinces of China had imported nine refrigerator assembly lines from an Italian company. All the nine lines were for producing Ariston refrigerators of the same 185 type with the same output of 10,000 sets each year. Some of the enterprises have made a profit after importing the assembly lines while others incurred losses; these losses are usually sustained by the provincial governments which took the decision to import the lines. But from the 'Framework' and other documents, we can see that the policy is changing, with more emphasis on domestic production of intermediate products, especially key components and parts of new products.

In short, the import regime in China today is on the one hand more liberalized than before, but on the other hand still biased towards protecting domestic industries. Therefore, it has two contradictory effects on the development of China's industry:

1. *Industrial diversion and upgrading effect* With protection, certain new industries have been established and the industrial structure has

been upgraded. Although in the short run this is obviously not efficient according to economic principles, its long-term effect on industrial development and overall economic development is hard to predict. Because of protection, some multinational corporations have entered China to share in this potentially huge market, while at the same time bringing in some advanced technology. On the other hand, the relatively liberalized import regime, together with the inflow of foreign investment and the rise of the non-state sector, has let consumers have a wider range of choice, and their choice will no doubt divert certain investment and production to those products that are welcomed by the market, and thus help change the industrial structure.

2. *Competition and price effect* With the gradual liberalization of the import regime, the import of foreign goods has forced the prices of many domestic goods down close to international levels, thereby exerting stronger pressure on domestic enterprises, which cannot survive market competition without raising productivity and efficiency. Moreover, there are nowadays many 'water' (smuggled) goods in China, a fact which also takes its toll on the prices of domestic counterparts. For example, though tariffs are still relatively high, prices of some durables such as TV sets, refrigerators and washing machines are almost the same as in duty-free shops for overseas Chinese and civil servants coming back from abroad. This kind of competition has forced China to produce goods with comparative advantage, a shift which is most obvious in its exports.

## The foreign exchange regime and industrial development

China's foreign exchange rate was fixed at an overvalued level before 1978. Since then, the official exchange rate had been declining and a *de facto* dual exchange-rate system was put in place first with an internal settlement rate and then with the establishment of a swap market, which reflected the equilibrium price of demand and supply. The dual-rate system was finally unified in 1994, taken over by a managed floating system. The gradual downward adjustment of the renminbi changed the relative prices of exportables and importables, and this had varying effects on export industries and import competing industries.

For export industries, it is clear that depreciation helped FTCs to cover the losses of foreign exchange earnings in terms of renminbi or to make them more profitable. Although the precise effect needs more careful quantitative analysis, there is no doubt that the depreciation of the renminbi promoted the expansion of exports. Even if the inputs of export industries were mainly from imports, the net effect would still be positive since their products were also for export. This is indicated by the rapid increase in exports, especially the increase in processed exports.

The impact on import competing industries should be examined more carefully. If the inputs of these industries depended mainly on domestic supply, they would not be severely hurt, because their costs and profits were not directly affected.[74] But if their inputs depended mainly on imports, the cost of production would rise and, other things being equal, the domestic prices of their products should also rise. They would be in a more difficult position to compete with imported finished goods. And yet this would force them to increase efficiency and eliminate inefficient enterprises. The net effect on import competing industries is therefore hard to assess. Statistically, if the increase in domestic prices of their products is smaller than the price rise of imported inputs after the depreciation of domestic currency, the net effect for import competing industries is negative; otherwise, it would be positive. However, dynamically, if these import competing enterprises were made more efficient because of the depreciation of the currency, the net effect could well be positive in the long run.

On the other hand, the depreciation of the renminbi hardly acted as a deterrent to China's imports. The fluctuation of imports, as pointed out earlier, is more or less a function of domestic demand rather than the price of the exchange rate. There are perhaps three elements in explaining this phenomenon. The first is that a large proportion of imported goods is used for processing exports. They would not affect the enterprises' behaviour so long as the wage rate did not change. The second is that some industries, supported by the state, could enjoy other

---

[74] Actually, other things being equal, the price of imported finished goods will rise, which benefits domestic import-competing industries.

preferential treatment, which would, to a certain extent, offset the impact of depreciation. The third is the continuation of inflation. The increase in domestic prices also partly offsets the price increase in imports owing to the depreciation.

## The effects of trade policy reforms on different types of enterprises

The above analysis has already mentioned the different responses of different enterprises to the trade policy reforms. Since China's economy is actually in a transitional period and the types of ownership of enterprises are also changing, it is necessary to look at the effects of policy changes across a range of enterprises.

At present, enterprises in China can be broadly classified into three groups according to their ownership: (1) state-owned enterprises (SOEs), including a large number of so-called collectively owned enterprises in the urban areas; (2) township and village enterprises (TVEs), which are mostly collectively owned; and (3) foreign-invested enterprises (FIEs) or foreign-funded enterprises, which can be further divided into joint ventures, joint management, and solely foreign-owned.

Tables 14.6 and 14.7 show that the GVIO produced by SOEs has increased at a much slower rate than that by non-state-owned sectors. During the fourteen years between 1980 and 1993, SOEs had only experienced two-digit growth in four years, while the non-state sectors all had two-digit growth in almost every year. The rise of non-state-owned sectors is phenomenal: between 1980 and 1993, the GVIO of SOEs increased only 4.80 times, while that of collective-owned enterprises increased 15.67 times, individual-owned enterprises over 55,000 times, and TVEs 45.03 times. FIEs are included in the entry of 'other' ownership, which also grew rapidly, over 217 times, during the fourteen years.

The effects of trade policy reforms on these different types of enterprises are not the same, because the production target, operational mechanism and institutional organization are quite different. First, the major objective for TVEs and FIEs is to earn profits, but this is not always the case for SOEs. Under the central planning system, the target for SOEs was to fulfil the Plan. Since almost everything was done

**Table 14.6: Gross value of industrial output of different types of enterprises (billion yuan)**

| Year | State-owned | Collective-owned | Individual-owned | Other ownership | Memo item: TVEs |
|------|------------|------------------|------------------|-----------------|-----------------|
| 1980 | 391.56 | 121.34 | 0.08 | 2.45 | 50.94 |
| 1981 | 403.71 | 132.94 | 0.19 | 3.14 | 57.93 |
| 1982 | 432.60 | 144.24 | 0.34 | 3.94 | 64.60 |
| 1983 | 473.94 | 166.31 | 0.75 | 5.04 | 75.71 |
| 1984 | 526.27 | 226.31 | 1.48 | 7.67 | 124.54 |
| 1985 | 630.21 | 311.72 | 17.98 | 11.74 | 182.72 |
| 1986 | 697.11 | 375.15 | 30.85 | 16.31 | 241.34 |
| 1987 | 825.01 | 478.17 | 50.24 | 27.88 | 324.29 |
| 1988 | 1,035.13 | 658.75 | 79.50 | 49.53 | 452.94 |
| 1989 | 1,234.29 | 787.51 | 105.77 | 75.84 | 524.41 |
| 1990 | 1,306.38 | 852.27 | 129.03 | 104.76 | 605.03 |
| 1991 | 1,495.46 | 1,008.48 | 106.91 | 159.96 | 870.86 |
| 1992 | 1,782.42 | 1,410.12 | 250.68 | 263.36 | 1,363.54 |
| 1993 | 2,272.47 | 2,021.32 | 440.21 | 535.21 | 2,344.66 |

*Source: Statistic Yearbook of China's Industrial Economy 1993*, pp. 35-6 (in Chinese); *Statistical Yearbook of China 1994.*

according to the Plan, enterprises had nothing to worry about even if they made losses, and they had little incentive to raise efficiency in production. When various kinds of contract responsibility systems were introduced after the reform, leaders of SOEs became more aware of profits, but their first task was still to fulfil the Plan, which usually set many targets, such as the increment of output over a certain period (usually three to five years), a certain ratio of profits and taxes to be handed over to the government, total amount of wages, etc. In exports, the major target for both manufacturing firms and FTCs is in terms of foreign exchange earnings. Governments of different levels will put pressure on enterprises to earn as much foreign exchange as possible without considering its real cost, because it is one of the important indicators of the performance of government officials, especially those engaging in foreign trade and economic activities. That is why the cost of earning foreign exchange in renminbi for most SOEs has in fact been higher than the exchange rate.

**Table 14.7: Growth rate of gross output value of industry (%)**

| Year | Total | State-owned | Collective-owned | Individual-owned | Other ownership | Memo item: TVEs |
|------|-------|-------------|------------------|------------------|-----------------|------------------|
| 1980 | 9.27  | 5.61  | 19.24 |         |       |       |
| 1981 | 4.29  | 2.53  | 9.01  | 134.57  | 31.60 | 13.72 |
| 1982 | 7.82  | 7.05  | 9.54  | 78.95   | 27.73 | 11.51 |
| 1983 | 11.19 | 9.39  | 15.53 | 120.59  | 33.90 | 17.20 |
| 1984 | 16.28 | 8.92  | 34.85 | 97.47   | 56.81 | 64.50 |
| 1985 | 21.39 | 12.94 | 32.69 | 1,114.86 | 39.54 | 46.72 |
| 1986 | 11.67 | 6.18  | 17.79 | 67.57   | 34.16 | 32.08 |
| 1987 | 17.69 | 11.30 | 23.24 | 56.59   | 66.39 | 34.37 |
| 1988 | 20.79 | 12.61 | 28.16 | 47.34   | 61.53 | 39.67 |
| 1989 | 8.54  | 3.86  | 10.48 | 23.77   | 42.68 | 15.80 |
| 1990 | 7.76  | 2.96  | 9.02  | 21.11   | 39.33 | 15.37 |
| 1991 | 14.77 | 8.62  | 18.40 | 25.29   | 50.11 | 43.94 |
| 1992 | 27.52 | 12.40 | 39.28 | 53.00   | 64.85 | 56.57 |
| 1993 | 28.02 | 5.73  | 35.96 | 67.97   | 86.54 | 71.95 |

*Source: Statistical Yearbook of China 1994.*

Even if profit is set as the most important target, short-term behaviour, such as exhaustive use of equipment and machinery to achieve as much profit in as short a period as possible without considering long-term investment and development of enterprises, can be expected and is not unusual. Under such a contract system, the situation is somewhat similar to (though better than) the planning system: the contract is actually a soft constraint, just like the soft budget constraint under the planning system, because even if the leaders of the SOEs cannot fulfil the contract, they can blame uncontrollable external factors such as price rises, so that usually they will not lose anything. But if they can meet the target, they enjoy a great deal of personal benefit. Therefore, the effects of the reforms, including the trade policy reforms on SOEs, are asymmetric: enterprises are responsible for their benefits but not for losses. When the renminbi was devalued and preferential policies were implemented, SOEs, also with certain protection, could survive and make profits. But when the subsidies were taken away, and import barriers were reduced, they suffered. The reduction of their shares in both exports and GVIO proves this.

**Table 14.8: Share of different types of enterprises in gross value of industrial output (%)**

| Year | State-owned | Collective-owned | Individual-owned | Other ownership | Memo item: TVEs |
|------|------|------|------|------|------|
| 1980 | 75.97 | 23.54 | 0.02 | 0.47 | 9.88 |
| 1981 | 74.76 | 24.62 | 0.04 | 0.58 | 10.73 |
| 1982 | 74.44 | 24.82 | 0.06 | 0.68 | 11.12 |
| 1983 | 73.36 | 25.74 | 0.12 | 0.78 | 11.72 |
| 1984 | 69.09 | 29.71 | 0.19 | 1.01 | 16.35 |
| 1985 | 64.86 | 32.08 | 1.85 | 1.21 | 18.81 |
| 1986 | 62.27 | 33.51 | 2.76 | 1.46 | 21.56 |
| 1987 | 59.73 | 34.62 | 3.64 | 2.02 | 23.48 |
| 1988 | 56.80 | 36.15 | 4.34 | 2.72 | 24.85 |
| 1989 | 56.06 | 35.69 | 4.80 | 3.44 | 23.82 |
| 1990 | 54.60 | 35.62 | 5.39 | 4.38 | 25.29 |
| 1991 | 52.90 | 35.70 | 5.70 | 5.66 | 30.83 |
| 1992 | 48.10 | 38.00 | 6.80 | 7.10 | 36.79 |
| 1993 | 43.13 | 38.36 | 8.35 | 10.16 | 44.50 |

*Source: Statistical Yearbook of China 1994*, pp. 363 and 375.

The same is also true for imports. Those SOEs that received approval to import various inputs would not pay attention to the efficient use of the imported inputs, as long as their import applications were approved and their products using these inputs could be sold. However, the relaxation of import control and the rise of non-state-owned enterprises had exerted greater pressure on SOEs. Many SOEs have the same characteristics of high cost and low efficiency. Their products are not capable of competing with imported goods or goods produced by FIEs. For example, it is said that the large importation of steel in 1994 forced down the domestic prices of steel, which led to one-third of iron and steel plants sustaining losses. Thus, the targeted import of steel in 1995 is said to be controlled at under 10 million tons with an additional 30 per cent tariff.

Because of low efficiency and high cost, SOEs' contribution to the national economy has steadily decreased in the past fourteen years. Table 14.8 shows that the share of SOEs in GVIO dropped from 76 per cent in 1980 to about 43 per cent in 1993. The most spectacular phenomenon is the expansion of TVEs. Though we have pointed out that there may be some statistical problems in calculating TVEs' share in GVIO, the quick expansion of TVEs is undeniable. In the early 1980s, the non-state sector was relatively small in China's industrial production and economy as a whole. In 1994, however, it accounted for about two-thirds of the gross national product and over half of its total value of industrial output.[75] Its share in foreign trade has now far exceeded 60 per cent.

Now, since the foreign exchange retention system has been eliminated and SOEs can no longer receive subsidies from the government, they are actually facing fiercer market competition. If there is no breakthrough in enterprise reform, the policy adjustment in foreign trade alone will not have much effect on the behaviour of SOEs. The liberalization of foreign trade has given a better price impetus to enterprises, including SOEs, and this, together with the rise of TVEs and FIEs, has put stronger pressure on SOEs. However, this external pressure will not automatically turn into an internal motive for improving efficiency. Actually, the losses incurred by SOEs have been on the increase. According to one estimate, as of November 1994, 41.4 per cent of SOEs made losses, and this was already 8.2 percentage points lower than the first season of the year.[76] Because of the heavy losses of the SOEs and thus the heavy financial burden on governments of different levels, especially on the central government, it was decided in 1995 to focus on enterprise reform.

Of course, not all the problems should be attributed to SOEs themselves. They really have some specific difficulties. One problem arises from the domestic investment system of SOEs, which still administratively allocate funds within the budget. This rigid system does not usually allocate funds to areas where profits can be maximized. The second problem is that many SOEs are very old enterprises with very old equipment and machinery that has not been written down in value for a long time. Thus, even if the new flow of capital could be directed towards the efficient sectors, the capital stock cannot be adjusted. Relatively backward techniques and technology also prevent the

---

[75] Ma and Liu, 1995.

[76] *Xinghua Journal*, No. 1, 1995, p. 57 (in Chinese).

improvement of efficiency. The third difficulty is that SOEs usually have a relatively heavier burden of wage costs. Because of the old system, enterprises must take responsibility for retired workers; old SOEs usually have a larger number of retired workers, whose livelihood depends on the growth of these enterprises.

Because of such difficulties, in 1996 the central government has stressed the importance of the reform of SOEs. It is obvious that, if they cannot make efficient use of resources and achieve effective management, they will either be elbowed out of foreign trade business or again be involved in heavy losses which will have to be covered by the state.

Unlike SOEs, TVEs and FIEs are not subject to the planning system and are basically profit-oriented, so they respond more sensibly to the trade policy reforms. Since China has provided various preferential treatments for exports, export industries, especially those enjoying comparative advantages in the international market, are relatively more profitable than their domestic counterparts. Many TVEs and FIEs would like to produce exports for the international market rather than goods for the domestic market. This is particularly obvious for processed exports, which can enjoy both import tariff exemption for materials and equipment and various kinds of preferential export treatment. This partly explains why processed exports increased so quickly and also why the relative contribution of TVEs and FIEs to exports has risen so fast.

TVEs are usually relatively small and labour-intensive, so they can enjoy a comparative advantage on the world market. Of course, TVEs are different from FIEs. Most TVEs have no rights to conduct foreign trade business, so they are mainly producing for the domestic market. But they are more flexible in dealing with FTCs and quicker in response towards changes in international markets than SOEs. Therefore, they are more or less in a better competitive position. The rise of TVEs has not only contributed a great deal to the national economy and exports, but also helped to solve the problem of unemployment. In 1993, the total labour force employed in TVEs reached 112.78 million, accounting for almost one-tenth of China's population.[77]

---

[77] Planning and Financing Section, Enterprise Department of the Ministry of Agriculture, 'Analysis of the development of TVEs in 1993', *China's Township Enterprises*, No. 10, 1994.

As for FIEs, there are usually two investment directions: one for export industries, and the other for import substitution industries. For those involved in export production, especially those in processing activities, the various preferential policy measures and their 'export enterprise' status strengthen their position in competing in international markets. Of course, not all FIEs are producing for exports. Some large multinational companies invest in China in order to occupy a certain share of this potentially large market. Here, the so-called 'advanced technology enterprise' status provides them with much preferential treatment. The relatively depressed domestic input prices and a cascading structure of nominal protection, in which tariffs increase at each stage of production, also helps this kind of production. These enterprises, aiming at China's domestic market, are relatively capital- and technology-intensive, and thus cannot, at the moment, enjoy the comparative advantage of China's cheap labour. However, by investing in China, they can avoid import barriers for exports to China and can enjoy a certain protection when producing and selling in the Chinese market.

Therefore, as regards the foreign trade policy reforms, SOEs are in a relatively unfavourable position compared with TVEs and FIEs. On the one hand, the relatively liberalized trade regime makes it more difficult for SOEs to compete both at home and abroad; but on the other hand, they cannot fully enjoy the protection the trade regime provides, since some FIEs are relatively more technologically advanced and can compete better than SOEs.

# 15 CONCLUSION

Trade policy reforms are on the whole a kind of liberalization, involving a process of decentralization and a reduction of mandatory plans. The liberalization of the trade regime has introduced more market forces and brought about stronger competition. On the export side, the reduction and abolition of subsidies and other domestic price reform measures forced enterprises to compete in international markets; on the import side, the change from direct administrative control to indirect control and the use of price mechanisms, and the gradual reduction of tariff rates and licences, have reduced import barriers. Imported goods and foreign investment have stimulated and strengthened competition in the domestic market. With the reforms and the rapid growth of trade, China's economy has become more integrated with the world economy. Of course, there remain trade barriers in China and the trade policy reforms still have a long way to go, but it cannot be denied that the reforms since the mid-1980s have had a great impact on China's trade and industrial development, and can be summarized as follows:

1. Trade policy reforms in China have in general been directed towards a more liberalized trade regime. The administrative planning system has gradually been replaced by a set of commercial policies such as tariffs and quotas. Although initially the level of tariff rates was high and a large number of tradables were covered by licensing, they have been gradually reduced, with tariffs playing an increasingly important role in regulating foreign trade.
2. The major objective of export policy is to earn as much foreign exchange as possible, so almost any item can enjoy preferential treatment as long as it is for export. The preferential measures have promoted the rapid growth of exports. While the import structure has

more or less remained the same, the export structure has changed from being relatively capital-intensive to being labour-intensive, with the striking feature of a rapid increase in manufactured processed exports. Since processed exports are mostly labour-intensive products, they have not helped to promote the upgrading of China's industry, but they have certainly contributed to the better allocation of resources, to rural industrialization and to employment. Although the emphasis has been gradually shifted to the export of machinery and electronics products, the value added in this kind of export is still low since processed exports constitute a large part.

3. The major objective of the import policy is still to protect domestic industries while at the same time supporting exports, so the import policy is more closely linked with the industrial policy. In order to support exports, imported materials for exports are exempted from import duties. In order to promote the upgrade of domestic industries, imports have always been composed mainly of capital goods and intermediate goods.

4. During the reform period, the industrial structure has been affected in two areas. One is the development of those industries that reflect China's comparative advantage and are involved in relatively labour-intensive processing activities. The development of these industries has benefited from the liberalization of the trade regime and is reflected in the rapid growth of TVEs and some small FIEs, whose contribution to total industrial output and total exports has increased greatly. The other area is the upgrade of industrial structure towards relatively more technology-intensive industries. This is directly affected by industrial policy, but it is also due to the inflow of foreign investment and the still protective nature of the trade regime.

5. But any analysis of the effects of trade policy reforms on industrial development should distinguish between state-owned enterprises and non-state sectors. Because of the inherent nature of SOEs and other factors, trade policy reforms cannot exert much influence on the behaviour of SOEs. But the effects on TVEs and FIEs are quite positive. With the opening up and changes in general and trade pol-

icy reforms in particular, TVEs and FIEs have developed very rapidly, and their contribution to both production and trade has increased very fast, while that of the SOEs has been declining. Since the behaviour of SOEs will not change simply in response to trade policy reforms, further reforms in external sectors without the simultaneous reform in domestic sectors, especially the reform of SOEs, might exert excess pressure on SOEs, whose bankruptcy could cause politically unacceptable social problems.

6. It is obvious that, at least in the short run, China will remain an exporter of labour-intensive products and importer of capital- and technology-intensive products. The further reform of trade policies will only strengthen this tendency, because this reflects China's comparative advantage. China has endeavoured to export relatively more capital- and technology-intensive products with higher value added, but even when it can do so, the products are mostly assembled with intermediate goods and inputs imported from abroad. Therefore, the assembly activities are still labour-intensive. On the other hand, since China has put stronger emphasis on industrial upgrading, the further liberalization of the import regime means larger imports of essential materials, technology, machinery and equipment, intermediate goods, and other inputs.

The further reform of foreign trade policies will promote not only the development of trade, but also the better allocation of resources. But to what extent China such reform will proceed depends primarily on two sets of conditions. One is the development of its domestic reforms. Of course, reforms in foreign relations have promoted, and will to a large extent continue to promote, the deepening of domestic reforms. On the other hand, since factor markets have not been developed and there has not been any breakthrough yet in reform of SOEs, trade reform will not gain much success without further reforms in the domestic sectors. If SOEs are still inefficient, if domestic investment is still administratively oriented, if factor prices such as wage rates and interest rates are still strictly regulated, if a social security system for medical care and retirement is not established, further rapid reform in foreign trade might even cause social chaos, producing an adverse effect on domestic stability and development. In short, while further reform in trade policy would be beneficial to China's trade and industrial development, it would need simultaneous reforms in other sectors.

The other set of conditions is the changes in the international market, and the reaction of the international community to China's reform in foreign economic relations. At present, the major issue is the negotiations for China's entry to the WTO. China applied to gain its seat in the General Agreement on Tariffs and Trade (GATT) in July 1986. The negotiations started in 1987 and have not yet succeeded, although the fact that they are still ongoing is a sign of China's willingness to integrate itself with the world economy. The issue has of course also caused much debate in China. Some economists and ministerial officials are afraid that the liberalization of foreign trade resulting from membership of GATT/WTO will allow many of China's industries to be exposed to too much international competition and thus endanger their survival, but most economists and government officials think it is better for China to join the WTO for both political and economic reasons. Although there may be short-term losses, the long-run benefits are much more significant.

Even so, more and more economists and officials are becoming impatient with the protracted negotiations. They think the major obstacles come from the United States, because it has pressed China too hard, requiring a developed-country status which is not acceptable. Actually, what China today agrees to accept is much more than the United States and other countries required at the early stage of the negotiations. But as China's economy develops, new demands have been made all the time. China is sceptical about the honesty of the United States in the negotiations but appreciates the EU's attitude, which supports China's entering the WTO. This was shown in its recent document 'A Long Term Policy for China–Europe Relations'[78] approved in October 1995. An alternative view, however, is that the EU does not openly object to China's entering the WTO because it knows the United States is taking the initiative in making demands.

---

[78] Commission of the European Communities, COM (95) 279, July 1995, OOPEC, Luxembourg.

The process of negotiation has no doubt exerted much pressure on China's liberalization of its foreign trade. Without the negotiation, China's foreign trade policy reforms would not have proceeded so quickly in the early 1990s. But if the negotiations are prolonged, this beneficial effect will disappear. Joining the WTO in 1996 would result in the further opening up of China and the extension of its foreign trade reforms; but if the conditions set by the United States and other countries are too high, this would only serve to delay further reforms in China's foreign trade policy.

# REFERENCES

*English:*

Fukasaku, Kiichiro and Wall, David (1994), *China's Long March to an Open Economy* (Paris: OECD).

Lardy, R. Nicholas (1992), *Foreign Trade and Economic Reform in China, 1978–1990* (Cambridge: Cambridge University Press).

Wall, David (1993), 'China's Special Economic Zones', mimeo.

Wall, David and Yin, Xiangshuo (1994), 'Technology development and export performance: is China a frog or a goose?', paper presented at a joint conference on technology transfer, Beijing, 2–9 April 1995.

World Bank (1988), *China: External Trade and Capital* (Washington, DC: World Bank).

World Bank (1993), *China's Foreign Trade Reform: Meeting the Challenge of the 1990s* (Washington, DC: World Bank).

Yin, Xiangshuo (1994), 'The effect of industrial policies on the exports of Shanghai', mimeo.


*Chinese:*

Chen, Huai and Jiang, Lin (1995), 'China's economic situation in 1995', *China Industrial Economy*, No. 1.

Fan, Baoqing (1994), 'China's foreign trade system close to international practice', *China Foreign Trade*, No. 3.

Guo, Lingsheng (1994), 'An introduction to the state import regulation system', *China Customs*, No. 7.

Ma, Hong and Liu, Shijing (1995), 'Some problems about the reform of state-owned enterprises', *China Industrial Economy*, No. 1.

Ming, Zhi (1995), 'Expanding machinery exports, developing machinery industry', *China Foreign Trade*, No. 2.

Ministry of Foreign Economic Relations and Trade, *Almanac of China's Foreign Economic Relations and Trade*, various years.

National Statistics Bureau, *Statistical Yearbook of China*, various years.

National Statistics Bureau, *A Statistical Survey of China 1991*.

National Statistics Bureau, *China's Economy in the 1980s* (China's Statistics Publishing House).

Sun, Shangqing (ed.) (1994), *China Market Development Report* (Beijing: Outlook Publishing House).

The Study Group of the Economic Institute, State Planning Commission (1993), 'The problem of dual structure and the economic development in the 1990s' (in Chinese), Economic Research, No. 7, 1993.

Yin, Xiangshuo (1993), 'China's foreign trade since 1989', in Guo Shiping (ed.), *The Analysis of China's Economic Situation Since 1989* (Hong Kong: Lizhi Publishing House).

Zhou, Xiaochuan (1990), *An Exploration of the Reform of the Foreign Trade System* (Beijing: Outlook Publishing House).